CONTENTS

As I've travelled and cooked across the globe, the main thing I've learned is that we all have a lot in common – it's the reason why so many ingredients cross borders.

Food and travel are my obsessions. I'm not a sit-on-the-beach traveller; I love immersing myself in different cultures, experiencing markets, finding produce and ingredients I've never seen before, eating roadside snacks, talking to street vendors, and 'staging' (working for free at restaurants), learning new techniques and cuisines. You name it, I'll do it!

I've been lucky enough to visit 46 countries (and counting), and each has made me appreciate the world we live in and our ability to connect with others through food. My favourite part of travel is coming home and creating a dish that allows me to share my experiences with others, and that's the heart of *The Atlas Cookbook*: a collection of 80 delicious, vibrant dishes inspired by 20 countries across four regions, celebrating the universal language of food.

Regional ingredients are the backbone of this book, but you won't need to kit out your pantry for each chapter – there are loads of crossovers (like eggplant/aubergine, bay leaves, white-wine vinegar) that are beloved all over the place. However, for some cuisines, one element is fundamental. Vietnamese food without fish sauce? Israeli cuisine without tahini? No chance! Enjoy experimenting with different flavours; you may even discover some new pantry staples.

While you might not have heard of all the ingredients, most are readily accessible. If you're having trouble with something like farofa (cassava flour) or za'atar (spice mix), try online or at speciality grocers or delicatessens. And just a note: I always use free-range eggs, and if the type of oil is not specified, it's grape seed oil (it's flavourless and has a high smoke point – I keep chilled olive oil for seasoning).

But just like travel, this book is about flexibility. Although I cook food from all over the world, I still have my own style, and when I get back into my kitchen recipes don't always turn out exactly like the dishes that inspired them. I like to let people know straight up that I can't compete with someone who has spent their whole life perfecting a dish when I've just visited a place for a week or two. As I cook, things get added or subtracted on the spot, and I substitute with what's in season locally (which is why each region in this book also aligns with a season). There have been many failures and successes, but I focus on the creative process: I try to use what I have, not set limitations, and allow myself to head off in a direction I feel best captures the experience.

In that spirit, don't be afraid to change up ingredients and expand on the ideas in these recipes. Most of the best cooking comes from mistakes and experimentation. I really enjoy plating things up, but you might like to be a bit looser in your presentation. If I say to dice the tomato and you'd rather leave them whole, do that! I've included ideas for substitutions, but use whatever's in the fridge. Each dish is easily adaptable to suit different dietary requirements. Meaty mains can easily be made vegetarian, and vegetarian dishes can be made plant-based. (You'll find that quite a few recipes are vegan and vegetarian already.) Treat this book as a guide or inspiration. Sure, follow the recipe to the gram if you prefer, but trust your instincts – if it looks ready, it probably is.

These aren't difficult, chef-y recipes, but they're not dumbed-down for the home cook either. Some might be challenging because they have four or five processes, but each process is simple in its own right.

Will you need fancy equipment? These are my big four: a mandoline for slicing things nice and thin, a microplane for zesting, a thermometer to measure oil temperatures, and a good set of kitchen scales. To me, these are essential in any kitchen, but the recipes can all be made without them.

Each dish is designed for four people to share. The idea is to make a mezze-style spread of dishes to create diversity and colour on the table for a casual get-together – nothing too fussy – where people can crack a bottle of wine (I recommend a big Argentinean red) and help themselves. I've given you some suggested menus on the next page as a starting point. You might need three to five dishes between four people, depending on your guests (and level of cooking enthusiasm), or you can always just make a couple of dishes and double the quantities. Many of these recipes also work for a solo midweek dinner (with leftovers for lunch the next day).

I want this book to inspire you to get creative, and to hopefully learn something along the way. Nothing excites me more than exploring the road less travelled, whether that's in life or in the kitchen. It's all about being open to new flavours and textures and embracing an approach to cooking that reflects the diverse world we live in.

SUMMER
Family Barbecue

NIBBLES

Kingfish Ceviche (page 37)
or
Clams with Avocado, Tamarind and Pineapple
(page 47)

Asparagus with Cheese Crackers (page 50)

BUFFET

**Grilled Tomahawk with Burnt Onion
and Chimichurri** (page 31)
or
Pork Chicharrones with Quinoa and Criolla
(page 43)

Cabbage and Uchucuta Coleslaw (page 41)
or
Corn and Chorizo Salad (page 17

Potato and Rocket Salad with Orange (page 27)
or
**Pumpkin with Spicy Salt
and White Cheese Sauce** (page 18)

AUTUMN
Mezze Feast

DIPS TO START

Signature Hummus (page 107)

Labne with Squeezed Tomato (page 89)
or
**Baba Ghanoush with Mint Olive Oil and
Savoury Halva** (page 98)

SHARE PLATES

**Raw Apple and Caramelised Walnuts
with Advieh** (page 101)
or
Zucchini and Rocket Salad with Dried Fruits
(page 102)

**Roasted Butternut with Red Onion
and Pepitas** (page 110)
or
Broccoli Tabouleh with Stem (page 90)

DESSERT

Knafeh (page 114)

WINTER
Long Lunch

SNACKS

Saganaki with Slow-cooked Onions (page 122)

Taramasalata with Black Olives and Pitta Bread
(page 121)
or
**Grilled Bread with Slow-Cooked Blood Orange,
Anchovies and Black Olives** (page 131)

ENTREE

A Simple Risotto (page 155)
or
Mackerel and Beetroot Niçoise Salad (page 162)

MAIN

Grilled Octopus with Garlic and Rosemary
(page 137)
or
Chicken Vin Jaune with Rocket and Carrots
(page 166)

Winter Roasted Greek Salad (page 127)
or
**Whole Burnt Cabbage Inspired by Vitello
Tonnato** (page 153)

SPRING
Weekend Grazing

Son-in-Law Eggs with Chilli Jam and Lime
(page 175)

Watermelon Salad with Peppered Pickles
(page 213)

Pipis with Ginger and Spring Onion Sauce
(page 216)
or
Prawns with Sambal and Pineapple
(page 193)

Wagyu Beef Pho Tartare (page 207)

**Whiting with Nuoc Cham Sauce,
Pickled Vegetables and Herbs**
(page 209)
or
**Pork Jowl with Tamarind Sambal
and Garlic Spinach**
(page 197)

Who the heck is Charlie Carrington?

When I quit school at age 15 to become a chef, my parents' reaction was, 'What the f*@#?'

I worked for a number of Australia's best restaurants (Stokehouse and Vue de Monde in Melbourne, Marque in Sydney), but after a few years I felt ready to get out of the kitchen and see the world. At the age of 20 I left for an eight-month round-the-world trip, spanning 15 countries, but after just one week, I felt hungry to get back into the kitchen again! So I ended up spending most of that trip 'staging'. I would email restaurants that excited me, and some of them let me spend time in their kitchens.

It was maybe the most defining period of my life. I was learning something new about food every day from an amazing array of chefs who generously shared their knowledge and culinary smarts with an upstart like me – whether that was in a hot, sweaty kitchen in Mexico, with orders I didn't understand barked in Spanish (bloody fun!), or in a month's stage at Restaurant Gordon Ramsay in the UK.

I returned home and went to work for Firedoor in Sydney, but I missed travelling and learning every day. So at the age of 22 I opened Atlas Dining in Melbourne, which completely changes cuisine every four months. Ups: being able to continue exploring my love of travel and new cuisines, winning a prestigious 'hat' from *The Age Good Food Guide* in my first year (and being the youngest to do so), and forming such an amazing network of friends and mentors. Downs: changing cuisine every four months is hard, as is trying to run a business with no idea. So why not open another one?!

Since then I've opened three Colours Bowls: casual mod-Israeli lunchtime cafes. I love how modern Israeli food is bright and simple, with spices blended from across the Middle East and vegetables allowed to be the star of the show.

About a month before the Atlas menu changes, I visit the upcoming country and go into research overdrive, eating six meals a day. It's intense, but I always come home bursting with inspiration and ideas (and all those meals), and with a whole bunch of new skills and knowledge. It keeps life interesting and gives me confidence to experiment with different ingredients and try new techniques. I hope this book will do the same for you.

COLOMBIA

ARGENTINA

SUMMER

PERU

BRAZIL

BOLIVIA

COLOMBIA

CAPITAL
Bogota

OFFICIAL LANGUAGE
Spanish

AREA
1,138,910 sq km

POPULATION
48,168,990

CURRENCY
Colombian peso

Fortifying soups, starchy tubers, fried plantains, wood-fired meats, cheesy street snacks and an astonishing array of tropical fruit. Colombia's cuisine is as diverse as its landscapes, from the tropical coast to the fertile interior to the Andean summits.

Three thousand kilometres of warm, humid coastline stretches along the Caribbean Sea and the North Pacific Ocean, offering a fresh supply of fish, lobster, pipis and other seafood. Head to Bogota, gaining 2640 metres in elevation along the way, for warming chicken soups, or visit Medellin and find beans, chorizo, avocado and tomato.

On the vegetable front, corn rules! It's charcoal-grilled with loads of butter and salt, simmered in soups, and turned into arepas (bready discs made from white corn). Unwrap Colombia's signature tamales, parcelled in corn husks or plantain leaves, and there's corn in there too, mixed with cheese, rice, meat – you name it.

Cassava, a root tuber, adds bulk to loads of dishes, and plantain (like a starchy banana with less sugar) is often served fried.

And geez do Colombians love their cheese: fresh, semi-fresh, stringy (like mozzarella), salted – cheese is a topping for, well, pretty much anything. It's also common in sweets, including as a side to hot chocolate – think of it like a biscuit: dunk and suck.

CORE INGREDIENTS

HERBS & SPICES
chilli, coriander

NUTS & SEEDS
sesame seeds

VEGETABLES
beans, carrot, cassava, corn, onion, peas, potato, pumpkin, tomato

MEATS & SEAFOOD
beef, chicken, chorizo, fish, lobster, pipi

FRUITS
avocado, banana, blackberry, dragon fruit, feijoa, gooseberry, guava, mandarin, mangosteen, orange, passionfruit, pawpaw, plantain, soursop, strawberry, tamarillo

DAIRY & EGGS
cheese, egg, milk

GRAINS & LEGUMES
barley, rice, tapioca

FATS & OILS
butter

SPECIALITY & OTHER
coconut, sugar

SUMMER

Corn and Chorizo Salad

Ingredients

180 g (6½ oz) chorizo, minced by hand

400 g (14 oz) corn, cut off the cob

½ bunch oregano, half chopped,
half leaves picked to garnish

20 green beans or runner beans,
cut into small pieces

100 g (3½ oz) spinach

150 g (5½ oz) Oaxaco or another white
cheese, pulled into thin shreds

The quality level of sausages can swing from fatty 'mystery bags' to artisan offerings made with top-quality meat. Same deal with chorizo, a dark-red mild or spicy sausage made with pork, pork back fat, annatto (a peppery spice also known as achiote) and smoked paprika. The more gourmet you go, the better the quality of the pork, the fresher the spices, and the tastier the sausage. Source quality chorizo from Spanish grocers, markets or delicatessens. Oaxaco – a white, stringy cheese – is actually traditional to Mexico. You can substitute it with another white cheese such as queso fresco (Spanish fresh cheese) or feta.

Method

In a large frying pan over a medium heat, cook the chorizo until it is crisp and golden, then set aside. In same pan, over a high heat, sauté the corn until it is slightly burnt. Add the chopped oregano and green beans and continue to cook, stirring occasionally, for 3 minutes or until the beans are just cooked. You want them to still be a bit crunchy.

To serve, scoop the corn mixture into a large bowl and let cool, then mix through the chorizo, spinach and string cheese and garnish with the reserved oregano leaves.

Pumpkin with Spicy Salt and White Cheese Sauce

Ingredients

½ pumpkin (squash), cut into large wedges

70 ml (2¼ fl oz) grape seed oil

1 tablespoon aji chilli powder

1 teaspoon garlic powder

150 g (5½ oz) queso fresco (or Danish feta or any crumbly white cheese)

50 g (1¾ oz) white crackers

juice of 2 limes

⅔ red onion, thinly sliced on a mandoline, to garnish

⅓ bunch coriander (cilantro), leaves picked, to garnish

Aji chilli is mid range on the Scoville heat scale and adds a warming heat to this dish, balanced by the sweetness of the pumpkin and the creaminess of the cheese. Eat this as an awesome vegetarian side or as a top-notch snack. If you can't source aji chilli, jalapeño works as a substitute.

Method

Preheat the oven to 200°C (400°F). In a large bowl, mix the pumpkin with 20 ml (¾ fl oz) of the oil and a small pinch of salt, then spread out on a baking tray and roast in the oven for 15 minutes.

In a bowl, combine a good pinch of salt with the chilli powder and garlic powder. After the pumpkin has roasted for 15 minutes, remove it from the oven and season it with the spicy salt. Return it to the oven for another 10 minutes.

In a blender blitz the queso fresco, crackers and lime juice together and check the seasoning. Spread the sauce on the bottom of the plate. Break the pumpkin up over the sauce and then garnish with the sliced onion and coriander leaves.

SUMMER

● VEGETARIAN

Corn Tamale with Shredded Chicken and Avocado Salad

Ingredients

1 tablespoon coriander seeds

½ teaspoon black peppercorns

2 bay leaves

5 garlic cloves

2 chicken breasts

50 ml (1¾ fl oz) olive oil

Tamales

250 g (9 oz) corn kernels

130 g (4½ oz) masa flour

120 g (4½ oz) vegetable lard
(such as Copha)

90 g (3 oz) aji amarillo paste (available
from farmers' markets or online)

4 banana leaves (optional)

Avocado salad

150 g (5½ oz) corn off the cob

50 ml (1¾ fl oz) olive oil

5 g (¼ oz) paprika

2 hard-boiled eggs, minced

½ bunch coriander (cilantro),
leaves picked, shredded

2 avocados, diced

juice of 2 limes

Masa flour is made from ground corn and used in a myriad South American street snacks, including Colombia's signature tamales. Masa (which is available from South America grocers) is mixed with all sorts of ingredients, typically corn, then wrapped in leaves or corn husks and steamed. Tamales can be labour intensive when starting out, but soon you'll be whipping these up in no time. If you want the fast, cheat-eats midweek version, leave the tamales out of this recipe entirely and replace them with an extra 200 g (7 oz) corn kernels in the chicken mix.

Method

For the tamales, in a blender blitz the corn kernels with 100 ml (3½ fl oz) water. Push the mixture through a fine strainer, then in a saucepan over a high heat bring the purée to a boil, stirring occasionally, until it thickens. Set aside. In a large bowl, mix the masa flour with 90 ml (3 fl oz) water, then combine in a blender with the corn purée, lard and aji amarillo paste. Divide the mixture between the banana leaves, wrap the leaves up like a parcel and steam them in a steamer for about 20 minutes or until they have firmed up quite a bit. If you don't have banana leaves or a steamer, preheat the oven to 180°C (350°F), spread the dough on a baking tray to about a 2 cm (3/4 inch) thickness and cover the dough with baking paper. Put a heatproof bowl filled with ice in the bottom of the oven, then steam the tamales in the oven for 40 minutes.

For the chicken, in a large saucepan bring 1 litre (34 fl oz/4 cups) water to the boil with the coriander seeds, peppercorns, bay leaves and garlic cloves. Drop the chicken in and cover, leaving on the lowest heat possible for 5 minutes. Remove from the heat and let it come to room temperature at its own speed. This can take up to 40 minutes. Once at room temperature, take the chicken out of the water and, using two forks, pull the flesh apart. Mix through the olive oil, just to keep it moist, and set aside.

For the salad, in a large non-stick pan over a high heat sauté the corn with a touch of the oil and all of the paprika. In a large bowl combine the corn, eggs, coriander and avocado and dress with the lime juice and remaining olive oil. Mix the chicken through the salad.

Once ready to serve, if you used the banana leaves, char the tamales in the banana leaves in a hot pan to burn them slightly. Open them up and add the chicken and salad mix and serve immediately. Otherwise, dice the tamale and toss through the chicken and salad.

Roasted Pork Belly with Pea and Onion Rice

Ingredients

1 kg (2 lb 3 oz) premium pork belly

400 g (14 oz) short-grain rice

40 ml (1¼ fl oz) grape seed oil

1 white onion, diced

2 garlic cloves, minced

1 teaspoon paprika

2 teaspoons salt

80 g (2¾ oz/½ cup) peas

40 g (1½ oz) spinach

40 g (1½ oz/⅔ cup) parsley

'Lesser' cuts of meat such as pork belly and lamb shoulder are part of the cool-kids gang at butchers these days, but it can be daunting to be faced with a thick slab of belly fat. Use the following technique of slow-cooking the meat overnight then blasting it at a high temperature for a flawless result and perfect crackling every time.

Method

Preheat the oven to 90°C (195°F). Put the pork belly on a baking tray and cook it in the oven for 10 hours (or overnight). Let it cool; the skin should be crisp and sound hollow when you knock on it. Raise the heat to 230°C (445°F). Return the pork to the oven and roast for 30 minutes until the skin crackles.

During that last 30 minutes, wash the rice in a strainer until the water runs clear. (This is the most important step!) Heat the oil in a large saucepan over a medium heat, and sweat the onion and garlic until the onion is translucent. Add the paprika and 1 litre (34 fl oz/4 cups) water, add the rice and bring to a rapid boil, then reduce to a simmer. Cook for exactly 15 minutes with the lid on. Then take it off the heat and leave it to the side, covered, for 5 minutes.

Remove the lid and fluff the rice with a wooden spoon – be careful of steam burns! Mix through the salt, peas, spinach and parsley. Turn the rice out on a serving platter, roughly chop the pork belly and scatter it over the rice to serve.

ARGENTINA

SUMMER

CAPITAL
Buenos Aires

OFFICIAL LANGUAGE
Spanish

AREA
2,780,400 sq km

POPULATION
44,694,120

CURRENCY
Argentine peso

Pasta and pizza in Argentina? You bet. Italian immigration in the late nineteenth century has had a profound influence on the national cuisine, as did the early Spanish settlers in the 1500s who brought recipes for spicy, warming stews, often found in the Andean north-west.

Argentineans are a carnivorous lot, earning a world-class reputation for their grass-fed cattle that once roamed the pampas (now they're mainly grown in feedlots). In recent years, disease struck Argentina's beef industry and the country is rebuilding its production.

Barbecue *(asado)* is a way of life, with long cuts of ribs, chorizo, sweetbreads and steak (or lamb and goat in Patagonia) cooked on a *parrilla* (grill) fired by coal or wood. It's considered an art form and a big cook-up often happens for Sunday family lunch.

Always served with barbecue is chimichurri, a garlic-loaded sauce with parsley, oregano, olive oil and vinegar, although each family and region has its own ingredient tweaks.

In the foothills of the Andes, Mendoza is Argentina's wine country with some of the world's highest-altitude vineyards at about 1000 metres. They are globally famous for producing stellar, sought-after malbec, along with cabernet sauvignon, tempranillo and chardonnay. Steak and a glass of red at 11 pm is classic Buenos Aires–style dining.

Dulce de leche (caramelised sweetened milk) is another renowned Argentinean treat, found in sticky treats such as alfajores, a magnificent shortbread sandwich.

CORE INGREDIENTS

HERBS & SPICES
bay leaf, cayenne, nutmeg, oregano, paprika, parsley, rosemary

NUTS & SEEDS
peanuts

VEGETABLES
corn, eggplant (aubergine), lettuce, onion, potato, squash, tomato, yam, zucchini (courgette)

MEATS & SEAFOOD
beef, fish, goat, lamb, pork, sweetbreads

FRUITS
apple, avocado, cherry, orange, pawpaw, peach, pear, plum, quince, strawberry

DAIRY & EGGS
cheese, egg, milk

GRAINS & LEGUMES
quinoa, rice

FATS & OILS
olive oil

SPECIALITY & OTHER
dulce de leche, wine

SUMMER

Potato and Rocket Salad with Orange

Ingredients

4 oranges

6 large boiling potatoes, peeled and sliced 1 cm (½ in) thick

70 ml (2¼ fl oz) grape seed oil

200 g (7 oz) rocket (arugula)

100 g (3½ oz) toasted almonds, chopped

Orange vinaigrette

100 ml (3½ fl oz) orange juice

50 g (1¾ oz) mustard

½ teaspoon salt

80 ml (2½ fl oz/⅓ cup) good-quality olive oil

½ teaspoon black pepper

1 shallot, roughly chopped

1 garlic clove, minced

This simple, rustic salad is a crowd favourite at every family barbecue. Why it works: bitey rocket (arugula) and tangy orange offset the creaminess of the waxy spuds, while the scatter of toasted almonds adds a nutritious crunch.

Method

First, peel the oranges. Segment the pieces of orange between the membranes and set aside.

Get a large, heavy-duty cast-iron frying pan and put over a medium–low heat. Toss the potato slices in the oil and place them flat on the pan for about 8–10 minutes on each side. Be careful not to completely overcook, but you want the potato to get some colour. Set aside and allow to come to room temperature.

For the vinaigrette, blend all the ingredients until fine and well combined.

Lay the potatoes on a platter and then spoon over some of the vinaigrette. In a large bowl combine the orange and rocket and arrange over the potatoes. Drizzle more vinaigrette on top and then sprinkle over the almonds and serve.

● VEGAN

Whipped Oregano Cheese with Roasted Vegetables

Ingredients

2 eggplants (aubergines)

2 red capsicums (bell peppers)

2 long green chillies (peppers), chopped

2 red onions, chopped

2 zucchini (courgettes), chopped

50 ml (1¾ fl oz) grape seed oil

60 ml (2 fl oz/¼ cup) Pedro Ximenez vinegar or a nice red-wine vinegar

40 ml (1¼ fl oz) olive oil

1 teaspoon salt

1 teaspoon paprika for dusting

Whipped oregano cheese

180 g (6½ oz) white cheese (queso blanco, or feta is acceptable)

1 bunch oregano, leaves picked and finely shredded (reserve a few leaves to garnish)

½ bunch thyme, leaves picked and finely chopped

40 ml (1¼ fl oz) olive oil

juice of 3 limes

Eggplant (aubergine), zucchini (courgette), capsicum (bell pepper) – the vegetable trinity of summer are the stars of this easy dish, while the whipped cheese creates the wow factor. Creamy, soft queso blanco is best but if you don't have a Spanish grocer handy, feta is a worthy substitute.

Method

Preheat the oven to 200°C (400°F). Put a wire rack over a gas flame turned all the way up and set the eggplants and capsicums on top. Using tongs to turn them, burn them on all sides. This takes about 8 minutes; don't be afraid to cook them until they are really burnt. Set aside.

Toss together the remaining vegetables in a roasting tin with the grape seed oil and roast in the oven for 15 minutes.

For the oregano cheese, whip all the ingredients together in a mixer with a whisk attachment, place in a piping (icing) bag or squeeze bottle with a large nozzle and set aside. (Alternatively, you can just spoon the cheese onto the plate when the time comes.)

In a bowl, whisk together the vinegar, olive oil and salt and set aside.

Once the eggplant and capsicum are cool enough to handle, peel them, discarding the skin and removing all the capsicum seeds. Roughly chop the flesh and combine with the roasted vegetables and the vinegar and olive oil dressing.

To serve, pipe the oregano cheese onto the plate and arrange the vegetables on top. Dust with the paprika and sprinkle over the remaining oregano.

● VEGETARIAN

Grilled Tomahawk with Burnt Onion and Chimichurri

Ingredients

4 onions

1.4 kg (3 lb 1 oz) tomahawk steak at room temperature

2 tablespoons olive oil

best flaked salt to taste

100 ml (3½ fl oz) sherry vinegar

50 g (1¾ oz) butter

Chimichurri

1 bunch coriander (cilantro), leaves picked

2 garlic cloves

¼ bunch thyme, leaves picked

½ bunch oregano, leaves picked

125 ml (4 fl oz/½ cup) olive oil

60 ml (2 fl oz/¼ cup) sherry vinegar

1 teaspoon black pepper

½ teaspoon salt

1 teaspoon chilli flakes

1 teaspoon dried oregano

1 teaspoon sugar

Go big or go home. Tomahawk steak, sometimes called 'cowboy steak', is rib eye with an extra-long bone left on so it resembles (you guessed it!) a tomahawk. It's a prime cut, and a chunk of grass-fed, dry-aged rib eye isn't cheap, so I tend to make this dish for special occasions. (A minute steak would make for a cheaper – and quicker – weeknight alternative.) It's a ridiculously tasty centrepiece, especially with chimichurri and Argentinean red wine!

Method

Preheat the oven to 200°C (400°F). Put the onions, skin and all, in a roasting tin and bake for 25 minutes.

While the onions cook, season the steak by coating your hands in the oil, then massaging it into the steak. From a height, sprinkle the salt very evenly over, then place on a massive pan, *plancha* or barbecue over a very high heat. Since the steak is so large and often pans don't have consistent heat throughout, it can be a challenge to cook the steak evenly. I find the best way to do this is to constantly rotate the steak by 90 degrees. After about 5 or 6 minutes, flip the steak and repeat on the other side. Remove from the heat and rest it in a nice warm place, either on top of the oven or near the stove.

Once the onions are cooked, cut them in half, still keeping the skin on. Use tongs to handle them, as they will be hot. Get a large frying pan very hot and, again using tongs, sear the cut side of the onions until blackened and burnt-smelling. Return the onions to the roasting tin, cut side up, and top each onion with the vinegar and butter. Put them back in the oven at 160°C (320°F) for 20 minutes.

For the chimichurri, pulse all the ingredients in a blender. You want a paste-like consistency – you don't want to purée it.

Return the pan or barbecue you cooked the steak on to a high heat, then reheat the steak for about 2 minutes on each side.

Place the onion halves on a large serving platter and pour some of the chimichurri where the steak will sit. Slice the steak and then season with more of your best flaked salt. Place it on top of the chimichurri, then drizzle over the remaining chimichurri and serve.

Braised Beef Cheeks with Carrot, Oregano and Red Onion Salad

Ingredients

2 beef cheeks

3 garlic cloves, crushed

1 red onion, roughly chopped

1 litre (34 fl oz/4 cups) beef stock

250 ml (8½ fl oz/1 cup) malbec

½ bunch thyme

2 bay leaves

Carrot, oregano and red onion salad

16 baby carrots, sliced lengthways on a mandoline

1 bunch oregano, leaves picked

1 red onion, thinly sliced on a mandoline

50 g (1¾ oz) dijon mustard

50 ml (1¾ fl oz) olive oil

20 ml (¾ fl oz) red-wine vinegar

Start this recipe a day ahead, or at least 10 hours before you plan to eat. You'll know you've nailed it when the meat easily breaks apart with a fork – no knife required. When making the sauce, be sure it doesn't catch or scorch on the bottom of the pan or the smokiness will destroy the flavours. Once the sauce is reduced to a beautiful syrupy glaze, add the beef.

Method

Preheat the oven to 110°C (230°F). In a large non-stick pan over a high heat, seal off the beef cheeks on all sides, then put in a roasting tin with a lid. Add the remaining ingredients, cover, and cook in the oven for 8–10 hours or overnight.

Remove from the oven and let it cool to room temperature, then strain the sauce and, in a large saucepan over a high heat, reduce it to a glaze. Add the beef cheeks to the glaze and keep on the stove over a very low heat, lid on, until you're ready to serve.

For the salad, in a large bowl combine the carrots, oregano and onion. In a small bowl whisk together the mustard, olive oil and red-wine vinegar, then dress the salad. Serve the warm beef cheeks alongside the salad.

PERU

CAPITAL
Bogota

OFFICIAL LANGUAGES
Spanish, Quechua, Aymara

AREA
1,285,210 sq km

POPULATION
31,331,230

CURRENCY
nuevo sol

Cuy (guinea pig) is a classic Peruvian dish, especially in the Andes, and over 60 million of these furry li'l rodents are eaten every year. They're delicious, served Peking duck–style with crisp, crunchy skin and mini pancakes, or grilled and deep-fried.

For the squeamish, don't worry, there's no guinea pig recipe in this chapter, but you will find one for tiger's milk. Thought to be an aphrodisiac, *leche de tigre* is jus left over from curing raw fish to make ceviche.

SUMMER

Peruvian food, like other South American cuisines, has been strongly Europeanised thanks to immigrants from Italy and Spain. There are traditional Peruvian staples of corn, potatoes, beans and quinoa (the vitamin B-rich pseudo-cereal grown at the foot of the Andes that is now a cafe staple worldwide), but there's also pizza and pasta too.

There was also a Japanese influx in Peru in the late nineteenth century, which created a Japanese-Peruvian food fusion dubbed 'Nikkei' cuisine. Fresh fish, treated as sashimi in Japan, was mixed with traditional Peruvian ingredients, such as corn and cassava, and lime and native aji chilli. I use yellow aji amarillo paste to make ocopa sauce (a spicy dressing) in my Burnt cauliflower (page 38).

CORE INGREDIENTS

HERBS & SPICES
basil, black mint, black pepper, chincho, cinnamon, clove, coriander, cumin, epazote, fennel, furikake, garlic, marjoram, nutmeg, oregano, paprika, parsley, thyme, togarashi spice mix, turmeric

NUTS & SEEDS
almonds, amaranth, quinoa, walnuts

VEGETABLES
aji chilli, artichoke, broccoli, cabbage, carrot, cauliflower, celery, corn, cucumber, eggplant (aubergine), lettuce, onion, potato, purple corn, spring onion (scallion), sweet potato, tomato

MEATS & SEAFOOD
beef, chicken, *cuy*, fish

FRUITS
apple, apricot, banana, cherry, cumquat, dragon fruit, fig, gooseberry, lime, melon, orange, passionfruit, pawpaw, peach, plantain, plum, prickly pear, quince

DAIRY & EGGS
cheese, egg

GRAINS & LEGUMES
barley, chickpeas, lentils, oats, pasta, rice, wheat

FATS & OILS
rayu, sesame oil

SPECIALITY & OTHER
banana leaves, cacao, carob syrup, fish-flavoured soy, honey, mirin, miso, ponzu, rice vinegar, sake, soy sauce, sugar, wasabi

SUMMER

Kingfish Ceviche

Ingredients

100 g (3½ oz) quinoa

360 g (12½ oz) kingfish, diced

8 baby cucumbers

8 baby carrots

1 teaspoon paprika for dusting

Tiger's milk

2 celery stalks, roughly chopped

½ white onion, roughly chopped

1 garlic clove

15 g (½ oz) fresh ginger

25 g (1 oz) salt

1 teaspoon sugar

50 g (1¾ oz) coriander (cilantro), stems included

10 carrots

100 ml (3½ fl oz) tomato juice

juice of 2 limes

2 tablespoons clear alcohol (preferably pisco, gin or vodka)

Tiger's milk, or *leche de tigre*, is the milky liquid used to cure raw fish for ceviche. It's a mix of lime, garlic, onion and salt. The trick is getting the balance right, so taste, and taste again – you might like more salt, another squeeze or two of lime, or maybe a smidge more ginger. Have fun with it! And relish in creating a dish that's authentically Nikkei.

Method

In a small saucepan boiling water over a high heat, cook the quinoa for 15 minutes, then strain the quinoa and blitz it in a blender. If needed, add a touch of water until it has the consistency of a purée. Set aside.

For the tiger's milk, in a blender blitz the celery, onion, garlic, ginger, salt, sugar and coriander to a pulp, then let it rest for 20 minutes. While it's resting, blend or juice the carrots, then strain into a small saucepan. Over a high heat, boil the juice until it thickens slightly. You'll need 75 ml (2½ fl oz). Strain the tomato juice through a clean tea towel (dish towel) until the liquid is clear, and set aside.

Combine the kingfish with the puréed quinoa and set aside.

Strain the blended tiger's milk liquid and discard the solids. Add in the lime juice as well as the strained tomato and carrot juices. This recipe is a guide, as so much goes into making this dressing, so check that it is sour, salty and full of flavour. Once the flavour is right, pour it into a teapot (or other pouring vessel) and set aside in the refrigerator.

On a mandoline slice the cucumber and carrots lengthways and store the slices in ice-water.

Roughly place the kingfish on the plate, then sprinkle over the carrot and cucumber and dust with the paprika. At the table, pour over the tiger's milk from the teapot to really impress your guests.

Burnt Cauliflower with Ocopa Sauce and Crumbled White Cheese

Ingredients

1 cauliflower

40 ml (1¼ fl oz) olive oil

120 g (4½ oz) queso fresco or feta (Danish, regular or even almond feta)

Ocopa sauce

1 heaped tablespoon mirasol chilli powder (or normal chilli powder)

1 heaped tablespoon aji amarillo paste

½ white onion, roughly chopped

1 garlic clove

75 g (2¾ oz) toasted peanuts

70 ml (2¼ fl oz) evaporated milk

75 ml (2½ fl oz) milk

60 g (2 oz) queso fresco (or feta)

30 g (1 oz) tostadas or crackers

This cauliflower makes an impressive vegetarian showstopper. Aji amarillo paste, often mixed with cheese, is a staple of Peruvian cooking, and adds richness and depth to a range of sauces, including ocopa. Aji amarillo paste and mirasol chilli powder can be sourced at farmers' markets or from online sellers of chilli peppers.

Method

Preheat the oven to 200°C (400°F) and cover a baking tray with baking paper. Find a saucepan large enough to fit the entire cauliflower, fill it with salted water and bring it to a boil. Submerge the whole cauliflower in the boiling water for 4 minutes. Using tongs, carefully remove it and place it on the prepared baking tray. Wait for the cauliflower to cool a bit, then rub the olive oil into the cauliflower until it is coated nicely. Bake it in the oven for 25 minutes or until slightly burnt on the outside.

To make the ocopa sauce, blitz all the ingredients except the crackers in a blender until smooth. Throw in the crackers at the end to thicken it; it needs to be thick enough that it will hold a shape.

When the cauliflower is done, go crazy splashing lines of ocopa sauce on the serving dish. Crumble the cheese over the sauce, then top with the whole cauliflower and enjoy. If you're really game, dig in with your hands!

● VEGETARIAN

Cabbage and Uchucuta Coleslaw

Ingredients

1 small red cabbage, shaved thinly

3 carrots, julienned on a mandoline

3 celery stalks, sliced

1 tablespoon salt

½ bunch mint to garnish

½ bunch spring onions (scallions),
chopped as thinly as possible
to garnish

Uchucuta

1 jalapeño, deseeded

1 small cucumber, roughly chopped

2 teaspoons black mint paste
(huacatay) or a few mint leaves

¼ red onion, roughly chopped

¼ bunch coriander (cilantro),
leaves picked

100 ml (3½ fl oz) milk

Bored with making the same old coleslaw? You won't be
with this recipe! Uchucuta, which means 'ground chilli' in
the Quechua language, is a vivid green, spicy salsa-like sauce.
(Tip: it's great to whack on fish, meat and eggs, so make
a double batch and keep some in the fridge or freezer.)
Huacatay (Peruvian black mint paste) is an amazing Andean
sauce that can be bought online.

Method

Combine the cabbage, carrots and celery in a large bowl,
sprinkle with the salt and leave for 15 minutes to soften
and draw out some water.

To make the uchucuta sauce, in a blender blitz the ingredients
to a fine purée.

Put the vegetables in a strainer and rinse with cold water to
remove the salt. Squeeze them out in a clean tea towel (dish
towel). Mound the vegetables on the plate, drizzle with the
uchucuta sauce, then garnish with the mint and spring onion.

● VEGETARIAN

Pork Chicharrones with Quinoa and Criolla

Ingredients

1 kg (2 lb 3 oz) pork jowl (cheek)

3 garlic cloves

40 g (1½ oz) fresh ginger

5 black peppercorns

2 star anise

2 cinnamon sticks

500 ml (17 fl oz/2 cups) grape seed oil

Quinoa salad

20 g (¾ oz) aji chilli paste

juice of 2 limes

1 garlic clove, finely chopped

2 oranges, 1 zested, both diced

60 ml (2 fl oz/¼ cup) good-quality olive oil

200 g (7 oz) cooked quinoa

1 zucchini (courgette), sliced into circles on a mandoline

10 pitted green olives, diced

60 g (2 oz) pepitas (pumpkin seeds)

Criolla salad

½ red onion, sliced and soaked in ice-water (this removes the astringent flavour)

1 tomato, chopped

½ bunch coriander (cilantro), leaves picked, chopped

Fried pork is enough to transport most carnivores to 'OMG!' territory, but this dish is easily turned vegan by ditching the pig and adding roasted zucchini (courgette). Either way you play it, it's a rockin' salad to have on the table.

Method

Preheat the oven to 200°C (400°F). Put the pork jowl in a roasting tin and bake for 30 minutes. While this is cooking, in a large saucepan over a high heat boil the garlic, ginger and spices together with 2.5 litres (85 fl oz/10 cups) water to create a quick stock.

Once the pork is cooked, pour the stock over and cover the tray with foil. Reduce the oven temperature to 150°C (300°F) and roast the pork for another 1.5 hours. Remove from the oven and leave it at room temperature to cool. Once it's cooled, break the jowl into pieces using your hands; it should be soft and break easily.

For the quinoa salad dressing, in a small bowl combine the chilli paste, lime juice, garlic, orange zest and olive oil and set aside.

To assemble the criolla salad, remove the onion from the ice-water, combine with the tomato and coriander and set aside.

In a large bowl combine the remaining quinoa salad ingredients and dress with the aji chilli dressing.

In a large saucepan heat the oil to 180°C (350°F). Fry the pork pieces until golden and crisp to create chicharrones. On a large platter sprinkle the quinoa salad everywhere, top with the chicharrones and then spread the criolla salad over the dish.

BRAZIL

CAPITAL
Brasilia

OFFICIAL LANGUAGE
Portuguese

AREA
8,515,770 sq km

POPULATION
208,846,890

CURRENCY
Brazilian real

Defining Brazilian cuisine is as tricky as finding a kangaroo in the Amazon. Party-hard Brazil is South America's largest country (a bit smaller than Australia in area) and has a crazy cultural mash-up of cuisines with hundreds of regional differences. I think it's one of the most underrated food countries in the world for its vast scope alone.

Indigenous ingredients combine with European influences, particularly from Portugal, Italy and Spain, to create warming seafood stews, hearty pork and black bean dishes, and snacks such as fried cassava chips or dried salt cod (*baccala*) to snaffle on the streets of São Paolo.

There's also Japanese inspiration in the form of ceviche, which draws its influence from sashimi, using chilli and lime. *Churrascarias* – barbecue restaurants – are found throughout the country, and you'll see Creole dishes from the southern USA and Afro-Brazilian food in the coastal areas.

In Salvador, right on the South Atlantic Ocean, I ate an amazing *vatapa* made by an incredible African-Brazilian woman. Vatapa is like a flavour-packed, creamy curry with peanuts, coconut milk, onion and garlic and garnished with prawns (shrimp) and capsicum (bell peppers), served with white rice.

CORE INGREDIENTS

HERBS & SPICES
coriander, grains of paradise, mace, malagueta pepper, pepper, sawtooth coriander (cilantro), tamarind

NUTS & SEEDS
almonds, brazil nuts, cashew nuts, peanuts

VEGETABLES
capsicum (bell peppers), chilli, choko (chayote), manioc root, okra, pumpkin (squash), sweet potato

MEATS & SEAFOOD
beef, octopus, pork, prawns (shrimp), salted cod

FRUITS
avocado, banana, buddha's hand, green papaya, guava, lime, mango, passionfruit, pineapple, plantain

DAIRY & EGGS
cheese, egg

GRAINS & LEGUMES
beans, polenta, rice, tapioca

FATS & OILS
olive oil

SPECIALITY & OTHER
cachaca, cane sugar, coconut, farofa, honey, tucupi, vinaigrette, yerba mate

SUMMER

Clams with Avocado, Tamarind and Pineapple

Ingredients

2 tablespoons tamarind pulp

lime juice and sugar, to taste

1 avocado, finely diced

2 tablespoons avocado oil

1 kg (2 lb 3 oz) clams (vongole)

50 ml (1¾ fl oz) cachaca (or another intense clear alcohol)

¼ pineapple, finely diced

Unless you're Brazilian, you mightn't have cooked with this combination of flavours before. This a fantastic dish to use common ingredients, such as avocado and pineapple, in a new way. Cachaca is a spirit made from fermented sugarcane juice, but if you can't source it, substitute white rum, which is made from molasses.

Method

In a small saucepan over a high heat, boil the tamarind pulp with an equal amount of water. Once it's the consistency of a thin purée, strain it. Check the flavour: it should be acidic and sweet. It may need a touch of lime juice and pinch of sugar. Set aside.

Dress the avocado with the avocado oil and set aside.

Get a large saucepan hot and add the clams and the alcohol. Put on the lid on and wait about 3 minutes until the liquid boils and the clams open. Carefully strain the clams and reserve the empty half of the shells for plating.

Place a small dot of the tamarind in each clam. Top each clam with some pineapple and avocado. Place the empty shells face down on the plate so the clams have something to sit on and serve!

Avocado, Bean and Burnt Kale Salad

Ingredients

2 avocados

100 g (3½ oz) cooked white beans

juice of 2 limes

40 g (1½ oz) tahini or almond butter

3 small Brazilian pimento chillies or
1 bird's eye chilli, deseeded

60 ml (2 fl oz/¼ cup) grape seed oil

1 bunch curly kale, shredded

120 g (4½ oz) toasted cashew nuts

coriander (cilantro) leaves to garnish

Bean salad

300 g (10½ oz) cooked black-eyed peas

1 orange, diced

½ red onion, diced

½ bunch mint, shredded

1 red capsicum (bell pepper), diced

1 teaspoon mace

juice of 2 limes

60 ml (2 fl oz/¼ cup) olive oil

This hearty bean salad has a bit of heat from the chilli, a nutty earthiness from the tahini, and a citrus zing from the orange and lime. It uses kale, an ingredient I love for its versatility. When you 'burn' the kale correctly it goes crispy, adding a special textural element to this dish.

BRAZIL

Method

In a large bowl combine all the bean salad ingredients and set aside at room temperature.

In a high-speed blender, mix the avocado flesh, beans, lime juice, tahini and chillies. Keep scraping down the sides to make sure it is smooth.

In a large non-stick pan over a high heat, warm the oil and toss all the kale in. The idea is to actually slightly burn the kale, then stir it through the salad. Roughly crush the toasted cashews in a mortar and pestle.

To serve, swirl some of the avocado whip on the plate, then pile some salad over the top. Roughly scatter the cashew nuts and coriander all over the dish.

● VEGAN

Asparagus with Cheese Crackers

Ingredients

100 g (3½ oz) Brazil nuts

24 large asparagus spears

60 g (2 oz) guava paste
(or fig, onion or guava jam)

75 ml (2½ fl oz) olive oil

juice of 2 limes

2 teaspoons salt

180 g (6½ oz) mild, firm blue cheese

60 g (2 oz) Danish feta
(or other white cheese)

2 tablespoons grape seed oil

flaked salt for seasoning

Cheese crackers

320 g (11½ oz) flour

65 ml (2¼ fl oz) olive oil

1 egg yolk

scant teaspoon salt

40 g (1½ oz) parmesan, grated

Guava paste, a Brazilian staple often eaten with cheese, harks back to the colonial days of Portuguese rule when guavas were used to replicate quince. In this recipe, I've used it to add sweetness. You can buy guava paste online or from a South American grocer. It's handy to have a mandoline for this recipe.

Method

Preheat the oven to 170°C (340°F). To make the cheese crackers, slowly combine the flour, 160 ml (5½ fl oz) water, 50 ml (1¾ fl oz) of the olive oil, the egg yolk and salt. Let the dough rest and pour over the remaining 15 ml (½ fl oz) of olive oil.

Shave the Brazil nuts on a mandoline to make little curls and reserve. Again using the mandoline, shave 4 of the asparagus spears into little circles and set aside.

Blitz the guava paste with 55 ml (1¾ fl oz) of the olive oil, 20 ml (¾ fl oz) of the lime juice and a pinch of the salt. Pour it into a container and then pour over the remaining 20 ml (¾ fl oz) of olive oil to help the mixture split.

To make the cheese sauce, blitz the two cheeses with the remaining lime juice and salt in a blender and reserve, preferably in a piping (icing) bag. (Alternatively, you can just spoon the cheese onto a place when the time comes.)

Next get a baking tray and flip it upside down. Brush it with a touch of oil, then place the cheese cracker dough on the tray. Using your hands, press the dough down to get it as thin as possible. Let it rest for a minute and then massage it flat again; the thinner the cracker, the better the dish, so take your time with this step.

Bake in the oven for 18 minutes, then remove the cracker and cover with the parmesan. Bake for another 4 minutes, then remove from the oven and let it finish cooking on the tray. Keep the oven on.

On a baking tray mix the remaining asparagus with the grape seed oil and give it a nice sprinkle of flaked salt. Roast for 8 minutes.

While the asparagus is cooking, break the cracker into plate-sized shards. Densely dot each cracker with the cheese sauce.

Pull the asparagus out of the oven and place on a platter, with all the spears pointing the same way in a line. Generously dress with the guava dressing, making sure to get some on the platter. Place the cracker shards on top to almost cover the asparagus, then cover with the thinly sliced asparagus and shaved Brazil nuts.

● VEGETARIAN

Warm Crab Scrambled Eggs with Polenta

Ingredients

8 eggs

20 ml (¾ fl oz) cream

80 ml (2½ fl oz/⅓ cup) oil

1 tablespoon annatto paste

2 teaspoons paprika

2 spring onions (scallions), minced

160 g (5½ oz) spanner crab
(raw weight, meat picked)

lime juice, to taste

100 g (3½ oz) farofa or 50 g (1¾ oz)
popcorn, blitzed to a powder

100 g (3½ oz) Brazil nuts,
shaved on a mandoline

Polenta

300 ml (10 fl oz) milk

1 bay leaf

1 garlic clove

1 teaspoon black peppercorns

1 teaspoon coriander seeds

1 teaspoon cloves

60 g (2 oz) polenta

20 g (¾ oz) parmesan, grated

Creamy scrambled eggs and soft polenta is a magical combo and this is a dish I've served time and again. It shows that eggs are not just for breakfast! Farofa is flour made from cassava (often called yuca), the tuber root of the South American shrub *Manihot esculenta*. It's a common ingredient in Brazil and can be found in Australia at speciality delis, markets and online grocers selling international food – but I've also suggested substituting it with popcorn powder (literally popcorn bitzed to a powder). Peppery and bright, annatto (achiote) paste can also be found at speciality delis or online.

Method

To make the polenta, in a large saucepan over a medium–high heat, bring the milk to the boil. Put the aromatics and spices in a heatproof bowl and carefully pour the hot milk over. Allow the milk to infuse for 20 minutes, then strain the milk, discarding the solids, and pour into a large saucepan over a low heat. Stir in the polenta. As it comes to the boil, remove from the heat and let it rest with a lid on for 10 minutes. Fold through the parmesan and set aside, covered, so it stays warm.

In a bowl whisk together the eggs and cream and then strain through a fine strainer and set aside.

In a small saucepan over a medium heat combine the oil, annatto paste and paprika until simmering. Carefully strain the oil and pour into a heatproof bowl and reserve. Heat a non-stick pan over a low heat with the egg mix and half the red oil. Fold the eggs slowly, and once the curds are set transfer to a bowl and set aside. Return the same pan to the stove, turn the heat up and sauté the spring onion. Add the crab and cook for around 2 minutes, just until the flesh turns white, then mix through the remaining red oil and eggs. Season with salt, pepper and lime juice to taste.

To serve, place the warm polenta on the plate, add the crab scrambled eggs and garnish with the farofa and shaved Brazil nuts.

BOLIVIA

CAPITAL
Sucre

OFFICIAL LANGUAGES
Spanish and 36 indigenous languages

AREA
1,098,580 sq km

POPULATION
11,306,340

CURRENCY
Boliviano

From the warm, welcoming people to the wild herbs ripe for foraging (and even the instant altitude sickness), I fell hard for Bolivia. The surreal, lunar-like landscapes near La Paz are the stuff of sci-fi, not to mention the lowlands of the Amazon Basin and the soaring Andean peaks.

Bolivian cuisine, like those of its South American neighbours, is a mix of indigenous and European (particularly Spanish) techniques and ingredients, along with influences from Japanese immigrants.

Potatoes, corn and quinoa are staples. Maize is used in drinks, soups, stews, and as popcorn, and quinoa, a nutrient-rich seed of the goosefoot plant native to the Andes, is eaten as a grain. Most meals are simple, centred on rice (the Spanish influence) or quinoa and spicy meat. A multi-course lunch is the most important meal of the day, followed by a siesta.

Between meals, pick up a deep-fried street snack of egg-and-cheese-stuffed potato, or get the party started with a glass of *chicha de jora* – beer made from corn!

At the restaurant I worked at in La Paz, we harvested springwater from a nearby waterfall (literally, filling the car with buckets) and foraged for herbs and flowers. On one of these trips I discovered 'mountain caviar', introduced to South America by the Japanese. From the *Bassia scoparia* plant, the pearly black-and-green seeds look like caviar and have a similar 'popping' texture. Finding and trying new ingredients is why I get up every day and this one was a culinary highlight.

CORE INGREDIENTS

HERBS & SPICES
coriander (cilantro), cumin, garlic, oregano, paprika, paprika, parsley, star anise

NUTS & SEEDS
chia, sesame seeds

VEGETABLES
cauliflower, chilli, corn, cucumber, lettuce, lima beans, potato, red onion, tomato, zucchini (courgette)

MEATS & SEAFOOD
beef, chicken, fish, pork

FRUITS
apricot, banana, date, fig, grape, grapefruit, lemon, lime, nectarine, olives, orange, raspberry, strawberry, tangerine, watermelon

DAIRY & EGGS
cheese, egg

GRAINS & LEGUMES
beans, quinoa, rice, wheat

FATS & OILS
olive oil, sesame oil, sunflower oil

SPECIALITY & OTHER
aji amarillo paste, chocolate, *chica de jora*

SUMMER

Burnt Sweet Potato with Puffed Quinoa, Quinoa Milk and Chives

Ingredients

400 g (14 oz) quinoa

4 sweet potatoes, halved lengthways

3 tablespoons vegetable oil

50 g (1¾ oz) fresh ginger, minced

2 shallots, minced

150 ml (5 fl oz) grape seed oil

juice of 2 limes

40 g (1½ oz) aji amarillo paste (available from farmers' markets or online)

300 ml (10 fl oz) oil for frying

1 teaspoon ground white pepper

1 teaspoon paprika

1 bunch chives, thinly chopped

If you're not confident puffing the quinoa, you could always buy puffed quinoa, otherwise just follow the directions for cooking the quinoa, then strain and fluff it up and season with the white pepper and paprika. It won't have that incredible crunch, but it will take some work out of the recipe.

Method

Preheat the oven to no higher than 50°C (120°F). Gently boil the quinoa in a large saucepan of water until you start to see little rings form in the quinoa. Set aside half of the quinoa for the quinoa milk. Spread the remaining quinoa out on a baking tray and dry it out in the oven until it returns its original texture, approximately 2 hours. Remove from the oven and set aside; raise the oven temperature to 200°C (400°F).

Thinly slice the sweet potatoes crossways, making sure not to cut all the way through to the flat bottom of each half. You want the potatoes to still hold together; this is known as hasselback style. Brush or rub the sweet potatoes with the vegetable oil and put them on a baking tray. Roast until fully cooked and a little bit burnt, approximately 1 hour.

While the sweet potatoes roast, in a small saucepan over a low heat combine the ginger, shallot and grape seed oil and gently cook, stirring occasionally. This process should take about 20 minutes; make sure it doesn't colour but it is cooked and aromatic. Remove from the heat and set aside.

For the quinoa milk, blitz the reserved quinoa with the lime juice, aji amarillo paste and about 150 ml (5 fl oz) of fresh cold water. It should be the consistency of a purée. Set aside.

In a large saucepan, heat the frying oil up until it's almost smoking. In small batches, put the baked quinoa in a strainer and dip it in the oil. Once the quinoa puffs up, carefully tip it out on paper towel, and dust it with the spices.

To serve, first spoon the quinoa milk on the plate. Brush the hot sweet potatoes with the ginger and shallot mix, place on top of the quinoa milk and sprinkle over the puffed quinoa and chives.

SUMMER

● VEGAN

Roasted Chicken Thighs with Spicy Herb Salad

Ingredients

8 chicken thighs, skin on

4 spicy red chillies

1 bunch coriander (cilantro),
half of it finely chopped

2 garlic cloves

juice of 1 lime

3 spring onions (scallions),
2 of them thinly cut on the diagonal

1 cos (romaine) lettuce,
broken into individual leaves

½ bunch parsley, chopped

Eat this as a standalone dish when you want something filling and flavourful without the carbs, otherwise the solo-serve lettuce cups also work brilliantly as part of a spread.

Method

Preheat the oven to 200°C (400°F). Put the chicken thighs on a baking tray, skin side up, and sprinkle on a touch of salt. Roast for 10 minutes.

In a blender blitz the chillies, the coriander that hasn't been chopped, garlic, lime juice and whole spring onion. Pour half of the spicy sauce on the chicken and roast for another 10 minutes.

Remove the chicken from the oven and let it cool slightly, then chop it with a sharp knife. Drizzle over the remaining spicy sauce and place the chicken in the lettuce cups with the remaining herbs scattered on top.

Potatoes with Trout Roe Cream

Ingredients

16 kipfler (fingerling) potatoes

1 garlic clove

1 teaspoon black pepper

4 eggs

200 g (7 oz) ready-made hot smoked trout, roughly broken into small bite-sized pieces

Trout roe cream

80 g (2¾ oz) trout roe

1 teaspoon salt

100 g (3½ oz) sour cream

juice of 2 lemons

I love fish-roe anything. This revamp of the classic fish–potato combo is so easy but it adds a dash of sophistication to any spread. Be warned – once this creamy potato-trout salad lands on the table, it's a fast mover, so don't expect leftovers for a midnight foray in the fridge! If finding trout roe is a problem, replace it with egg yolk, but the cream's consistency will be more like mayo and not as fishy.

BOLIVIA

Method

Put the potatoes, garlic and black pepper in a large saucepan and cover with plenty of cold water. Boil for 20 minutes, then remove from the heat and allow to cool.

While the potatoes are boiling, bring a small saucepan of water to the boil. Set aside a bowl of ice-water. Put the eggs in the boiling water for 8 minutes, then refresh in the ice-water. Peel them under water – the water helps separate the shell from the white, making them easier to peel. Then, using a grater or potato masher, push the eggs through to get a coarse texture and set aside.

To make the trout egg cream, combine all the ingredients in a large mixing bowl and check the seasoning.

To serve, place the trout egg cream on the plate, top with the room-temperature potatoes followed by the minced egg and broken hot smoked trout.

Grilled Pork Chops with Black-eyed Peas, Grapefruit and Cashew Nuts

Ingredients

300 g (10½ oz) cooked black-eyed peas

4 pork chops

3 grapefruits, segmented and juice reserved

½ red onion, sliced

100 g (3½ oz/⅔ cup) cashew nuts

20 ml (¾ fl oz) olive oil

The mild pork taste and creamy texture of black-eyed peas is a long-loved flavour combo in South America and the south of the USA, appearing often on soul food menus. Here, the puréed legume makes a warming base for the tender meat, while the bright, citrus tang and sharp onion add colour and kick.

Method

Blitz the cooked black-eyed peas in a blender with 250 ml (8½ fl oz) water and salt to taste. Once blended, put the purée in a small saucepan over a very low heat.

In a large non-stick pan sear the pork chops over a high heat. If your pan isn't big enough, do two at once and set them aside to rest while you do the other two. They should be seared for about 4 minutes on each side, rested for about 6 minutes, then flash-fried again just before serving.

While the pork is resting, in a bowl combine the grapefruit, onion and cashew nuts with the olive oil and grapefruit juice.

Slice the pork. Place the warm bean purée on the plate, top it with the pork and then pile the salad to the side.

TURKEY

SYRIA

AUTUMN

LEBANON

IRAQ

ISRAEL

TURKEY

CAPITAL
Istanbul

OFFICIAL LANGUAGE
Turkish

AREA
783,560 sq km

POPULATION
81,257,240

CURRENCY
Turkish lira

AUTUMN

Wedged between Europe and the Middle East, and bordering the Mediterranean and Black Sea, Turkey is a fantastic country to eat your way around.

Wherever you travel, whether you're sampling gozleme in Anatolia, exploring the Aegean olive groves, or scoffing street snacks in Istanbul, one thing is clear: Turks love their food.

They're an extremely sociable bunch, especially after a couple of rakis (the boozy, anise-flavoured spirit), and shareable family feasts are essential to their way of life.

Turkish cuisine is largely the legacy of the Ottomans, and mezze, a collection of small salads or dips to be shared around the table, is a typical way to eat. *Corba* (soup), such as lentil or yoghurt, is usually eaten at the start of a meal.

The Turks are fiercely seasonal cooks, and dishes may swing from wild-caught fish (best eaten while enjoying Black Sea vistas); spicy, skewered charcoal-grilled meats; or freshly harvested vegetables, such as artichokes and green beans.

Istanbul, a key player in the spice trade, has its famous spice bazaar, with souks selling sumac, coriander, and isot, a Kurdish black pepper with a unique chocolatey flavour and mild heat. These precious ingredients are incredibly fresh, full of colour, and bursting with aroma.

Traditional Tulum cheese, made from goat's milk and hung in goat's skin in cool caves, is a speciality worth seeking out, and don't forget the yoghurt! A household staple, it's eaten plain, as a side, and in soups, mains and drinks.

CORE INGREDIENTS

HERBS & SPICES
allspice, aniseed, black pepper, cardamom, cinnamon, clove, coriander, cumin, fenugreek, garlic, isot, mastic, saffron, sumac

NUTS & SEEDS
almonds, hazelnuts, nigella seeds, peanuts, pistachio nuts, poppy seeds, sesame seeds, walnuts

VEGETABLES
artichoke, cabbage, capsicum (bell pepper), carrot, cauliflower, celery, eggplant (aubergine), green beans, Jerusalem artichoke, leek, okra, onion, spinach, string beans, tomato, zucchini (courgette)

MEATS & SEAFOOD
chicken, lamb, fish

FRUITS
apple, apricot, fig, grape, pear, plum, pomegranate

DAIRY & EGGS
cottage cheese, egg, Tulum cheese, yoghurt

GRAINS & LEGUMES
chickpeas, lentils, rice, wheat

FATS & OILS
butter, canola oil, olive oil, sunflower oil

SPECIALITY & OTHER
grape leaves, raki, rosewater

AUTUMN

Coskun's Cilbir

Ingredients

200 g (7 oz) yoghurt

30 g (1 oz) smoking chips

200 g (7 oz) butter, diced

pinch of sumac

small pinch of salt

150 g (5½ oz) raw chicken skin

50 g (1¾ oz) milk powder

2 tablespoons white vinegar

4 eggs

2 large pitta breads,
cut into triangles, to serve

Cilbir is a rusted-on Turkish menu item – records show Ottoman sultans tucking into it as early as the fifteenth century. This recipe comes from my mentor and buddy, Turkish chef Coskun Uysal. Cilbir was his favourite after-school snack, proving a great brunch dish isn't bound by the confines of time. He's given it a modern revamp with brown butter crumble and crisp chicken skin. If you are time poor, you can skip smoking the yoghurt. Smoking chips are available at all good kitchen supply stores.

Method

For the smoked yoghurt, spread the yoghurt out on a flat tray and chill it in the fridge for 30 minutes. While you are preparing the smoking set-up, put the yoghurt in a cold oven on the top shelf. Get a cast-iron pan hot, then sprinkle in the smoking chips. With a match, light the chips on fire, then put a lid on the pan to kill the fire. Remove the lid, place the pan under the yoghurt and shut the oven door. Leave it for 10 minutes to give that fantastic smoky flavour, then refrigerate until needed.

Put half the diced butter into a saucepan and bring to a high heat, whisking constantly, until it goes golden and smells nutty. Stir in the sumac and salt and then carefully pour into a heatproof bowl and set aside.

Preheat the oven to 180°C (350°F). On a clean work surface lay the chicken skin out flat and scrape off any additional fat using a blunt knife. Place it in between 2 sheets of baking paper, press it between two baking trays and bake in the oven for 25 minutes. Remove from the oven and, when cool enough to handle, break up into large shards.

In the same saucepan you browned the butter, over a medium heat cook the remaining butter with the milk powder until it becomes darker in colour and resembles a crumble. Remove from the heat and set aside.

Now to poach the eggs. Poaching eggs is extremely easy, but you need to have confidence! Fill a large saucepan with water, bring it to the boil and pour in the vinegar. Crack the eggs into the water and then simmer for about 2.5 to 3 minutes, then remove using a slotted spoon and set aside on paper towel.

Put a smear of cold yoghurt in the middle of the bowl and place the egg on top. Cover with the brown butter crumble, add shards of chicken skin on top, pour the sumac butter over and then serve immediately with the pitta on the side.

Salt-baked Kohlrabi with Caramelised Onion Yoghurt and Poppy Seeds

Ingredients

200 g (7 oz) rock salt

2 kohlrabi

3 onions, thinly sliced

2 tablespoons grape seed oil

2 teaspoons sugar

1 teaspoon sumac

juice of 1 lemon

150 g (5½ oz) yoghurt

2 tablespoons poppy seeds, plus extra to garnish

2 tablespoons chopped chives

2 tablespoons almonds, chopped or crushed in a mortar and pestle

½ teaspoon cumin

Salt-baking is a fantastic – and fun – technique traditional to many cultures, including those of Turkey, China and southern Italy. The idea is to create a hard crust, like a bespoke baking dish, that steams and seals the flavours. Roasting on rock salt is a simpler method, giving the same flavour-packed result. But if you do want to make salt dough, mix one part salt, one part flour and one part water until it's the consistency of wet sand, bury your food in it (fish and potatoes work well too), and bake. When it's done, crack the crust and dig in.

Method

Preheat the oven to 180°C (350°F). Cover a baking tray with the rock salt and put the kohlrabi on top. Cover the tray with foil and bake for 45 minutes.

Put the onions and oil in a frying pan with a tight-fitting lid. Cook over a low heat and leave the lid on for 15 minutes to let the onions sweat. Remove the lid, add the sugar and stir. Let the moisture evaporate and the onions go a dark golden brown. Remove from the heat and let cool to room temperature, then mix in half the sumac, the lemon juice and yoghurt and check the seasoning. Set aside.

In a bowl combine the poppy seeds, chives, almonds and cumin.

Once the kohlrabi is cooked, using tongs burn the skin over an open flame, then halve it and scoop out the flesh, reserving the burnt skin. Roughly chop the flesh then fold through the poppy seed mix.

Put the burnt skin on the plate then pile everything on top like a salad. Spoon over the caramelised onion yoghurt, remaining sumac and extra poppy seeds to serve.

● VEGETARIAN

Cauliflower Couscous with Sunflower Kernels

Ingredients

1 cauliflower

280 g (10 oz) sunflower kernels, 100 g (3½ oz) toasted

90 ml (3 fl oz) olive oil

80 g (2¾ oz) tahini

seeds of 1 pomegranate

½ teaspoon cumin

2 red apples, diced

juice of 1 lemon

Ah cauliflower, the chameleon of the vegetable world. I love how this hearty brassica can star in a salad, be the hero of a main, or add depth to a mezze as a tasty side. Its versatility is its strength, and for this reason it's widely used across Turkey. Using a humble grater, this easy-pleaser recipe gives cauliflower a couscous-like texture, making it a healthy, robust option for a salad base.

Method

Preheat the oven to 200°C (400°F). Half-fill a saucepan big enough to fit half a cauliflower with salted water and bring to the boil. Halve the cauliflower through the core. Drop one half of the cauliflower in the boiling water for 3 minutes, then remove and let air dry. (Keep the saucepan of salted water to the side – you'll use it later in this recipe.) Rub your hands with a tablespoon or two of the olive oil and massage it into the cauliflower, then put it on a baking tray and roast it in the oven for 25 minutes. It should be slightly burnt when it's done.

In a blender blitz together the untoasted sunflower kernels, 60 ml (2 fl oz) of the olive oil and the tahini and set aside.

To make the cauliflower couscous, grate the remaining cauliflower half, excluding the stem, using a semi-fine grater. Once the roasted cauliflower is almost ready, return the saucepan of salted water to the boil then quickly blanch the couscous for 10 seconds. Strain the couscous, fold through the rest of the ingredients and season to taste with salt.

Quarter the roasted cauliflower through the stem and place on top of the couscous. Drizzle with the tahini sauce to serve.

VEGAN

Seared Lamb 'Kofte' Tartare with Celeriac and Walnut Tarator

Ingredients

2 premium lamb rumps up to 1 kg (2 lb 3 oz) total

60 ml (2 fl oz) grape seed oil

1 onion, diced

2 garlic cloves, minced

½ teaspoon coriander seeds

½ teaspoon ground ginger

½ teaspoon paprika, plus extra to garnish

1 teaspoon cumin

⅓ bunch mint, finely shredded

⅓ bunch parsley, finely shredded

100 g (3½ oz) rock salt

1 small celeriac, peeled with a sharp knife

50 g (1¾ oz) butter

Walnut tarator

70 g (2½ oz) puréed fresh walnuts (walnut butter)

130 g (4½ oz) yoghurt

1 garlic clove

60 g (2 oz) tahini

⅓ bunch parsley, finely shredded

'Can I really make tartare at home?' you might be wondering. Yes! Yes, you can! It's safe, easy and bloody delicious. The trick is using top-quality meat. My take on 'kofte' is inspired by Turkey's classic grilled lamb skewers. I've used a similar spice profile, but kept the meat on the raw side of rare, which gives it an amazing buttery flavour. Team that with salt-baked celeriac and walnut tarator – an easy, garlicky, yoghurt-tahini sauce – for extra oomph.

Method

Using a knife take most of the lamb skin off and discard and remove any silver skin, slice into 1 cm (½ in) thick pieces and leave at room temperature.

Heat 40 ml (1¼ fl oz) of the oil in a saucepan over a medium–low heat, and add the onion and garlic. Sweat it, but don't get any colour on it. Once it's translucent, add in all the spices and set to the side to cool. Once it has cooled, fold through the herbs.

Preheat the oven to 200°C (400°F). To salt-bake the celeriac, layer the salt on a baking tray and then cover with a sheet of baking paper. Put a few really thin slashes through the paper so the salt can slightly seep through. Top with the celeriac then cover the tray with foil and roast in the oven for 50 minutes.

To make the tarator, in a blender blitz everything but the parsley together with 2 tablespoons water until it is starting to get smooth but is still textured, then fold through the parsley and set aside.

When the celeriac is roasted, in a large non-stick frying pan over a medium–high heat, melt the butter and remaining oil and add the celeriac. Using a lid that is smaller than the pan, press the celeriac down and sear it until it colours on one side, then turn the heat off and let it continue to cook in the pan.

To prepare the lamb, get a hot griddle or large frying pan very hot and, in batches so you don't overload the griddle, quickly sear the lamb slices on one side. This should take 30 seconds. Remove from the pan, then dice. Season this with the onion, spice and herb mix.

To serve, spoon the tarator on the plate then loosely place the tartare. Roughly chop the celeriac, then arrange it, golden side up, on one side of the plate. Dust with paprika and enjoy!

SYRIA

CAPITAL
Damascus

OFFICIAL LANGUAGE
Arabic

AREA
185,180 sq km

POPULATION
18,284,410

CURRENCY
Syrian pound

Syria is experiencing horrific political and social upheaval. Without trivialising the situation in any way, I'd like to focus on Syria's food and culinary traditions. In this food-loving country, many recipes are handed down from the thirteenth century and people typically eat in mezze-style feasts.

Eggplants (aubergines) are a menu favourite – stuffed, fried, moussaka-ed or turned into dip. Broad (fava) beans are eaten at breakfast, lunch and dinner, and nutty, honey-sticky sweets with their distinctive hit of rosewater are typical street foods of Damascus.

Syrians love the bite of salty cheeses, such as feta and shanklish (a sheep's milk cheese covered in za'atar and other spices, available from Middle Eastern grocers) and the sour tang of yoghurt and labne.

Ancient spices – cinnamon, cardamom, ground turmeric – are used to flavour meat for Syria's famous shawarma, and delicate, velvety sweetbreads can be found in certain dishes, including my recipe for potato salad (page 83).

CORE INGREDIENTS

HERBS & SPICES
aleppo pepper, cardamon, cinnamon, garlic, mint, turmeric

NUTS & SEEDS
pistachio nuts, sesame seeds

VEGETABLES
cabbage, cauliflower, cucumber, eggplant (aubergine), tomato, zucchini (courgette)

MEATS & SEAFOOD
lamb, sweetbreads

FRUITS
cherry, date, lemon

DAIRY & EGGS
feta, haloumi, shanklish, yoghurt

GRAINS & LEGUMES
broad (fava) beans, burghul (bulgur wheat), chickpeas, freekeh, lentils, rice

FATS & OILS
olive oil

SPECIALITY & OTHER
honey, pickled turnips, rosewater, vine leaves

AUTUMN

Runner Beans with Olive Oil, Lemon Juice and Garlic

Ingredients

800 g (1 lb 12 oz) runner beans

2 tablespoons grape seed oil

3 garlic cloves, grated then minced finely

juice of 2 lemons

80 ml (2½ fl oz/⅓ cup) olive oil

flaked salt, to garnish

Watch your guests go berserk over beans. This no-fail Syrian staple is ridiculously good and an absolute favourite for its sheer simplicity. I love how one ingredient can have so much impact. The key is to get a lot of colour on the beans prior to tossing in the dressing. If you can't find runner beans, use green beans – but remember, they'll cook faster. Smash a bowl of these as you would hot chips, eat them with flatbread and labne, or try them cold the next day as a lunchy leftover.

Method

Heat up a griddle or preferably a charcoal grill. Coat the beans in the oil and then place the beans on the highest heat possible and burn one side, then the other. Immediately remove from the heat, put in a bowl and toss in the garlic, lemon juice and olive oil. If you used runner beans, it looks great to lie them all next to each other neatly. Salt and serve!

● VEGAN

Falafel with Mint Tahini

Ingredients

1 litre (34 fl oz/4 cups) frying oil

450 g (1 lb) chickpeas, soaked for a minimum of 8 hours (preferably overnight)

100 g (3½ oz) spinach

½ bunch coriander (cilantro), leaves picked

1 bunch parsley, leaves picked

2 medium shallots, diced

2 garlic cloves

large pinch of ground coriander

large pinch of cumin

large pinch of ground black pepper

3 tablespoons flour

Mint tahini

120 g (4½ oz) tahini

juice of 2 lemons

1 bunch mint, leaves picked, some reserved for garnish

The battle for credit over who invented falafel is real: many countries claim ownership of this beloved Middle Eastern street snack. Egypt is widely acknowledged as the frontrunner, with Syria a close second. Wherever its origins, it's the ultimate vego comfort food and a top-notch recipe to have in your repertoire. The trick is to soak the chickpeas first (ideally overnight), blitz the other ingredients separately, and *then* fold in the chickpeas. That way, you'll have textural, vibrantly green falafel every time.

Method

Strain the soaked chickpeas and grind them down to a sandy texture in a food processor, then scrape out into a large mixing bowl. Add the remaining ingredients except for the flour to the blender and purée. Pour this vibrant green purée over the chickpeas, followed by the flour, and then combine well. Check the seasoning while it's raw – it should already be tasty.

To make the mint tahini, blitz everything together with 120 ml (4 fl oz) water and season with some salt. Pour it into a squeeze bottle and set aside. (Alternatively, you can just spoon the tahini onto a plate when the time comes.)

Add the oil to a stockpot large enough that the oil won't overflow when you add the falafel. Heat the oil to 180°C (350°F). Be very careful when frying the falafel – even the most experienced chefs can burn themselves! Using an ice cream scoop (ideally one that you can squeeze to release what you've scooped), scoop the falafel mix and gently place it in the oil, carefully flicking the scoop to knock the falafel off. If that feels too dangerous, scoop the falafel onto a spider utensil to avoid spattering, then place it in the hot oil. Fry until golden, around 4 minutes.

Squeeze the mint tahini onto the plate in crazy graffiti-like squiggles, and then put as many falafels as possible on the plate they will all be eaten! Cover with the fresh mint and enjoy.

● VEGAN

81

Mint Potatoes with Sweetbreads and Herb and Onion Salad

Ingredients

600 g (1 lb 5 oz) small potatoes

60 ml (2 fl oz/¼ cup) grape seed oil

1 bunch mint, shredded

½ bunch coriander (cilantro), leaves picked

½ bunch parsley, leaves picked

½ bunch dill, fronds picked

1 white onion, thinly sliced and soaked in ice-water then dried on paper towel (this removed the astringent flavour)

20 ml (¾ fl oz) olive oil

juice of 2 lemons

1 teaspoon za'atar

150 g (5½ oz) butter

3 garlic cloves, minced

500 g (1 lb 2 oz) veal sweetbreads

¼ bunch thyme, leaves picked

If offal makes you squeamish, this dish might help you get over it! Veal sweetbreads (the gland from the thymus or pancreas) are prized for their mild, velvety texture and they ramp up the flavour of this dish big time. You can make your own za'atar – a spice blend of sesame seeds and herbs – or buy it at spice shops or Middle Eastern grocers.

Method

Preheat the oven to 190°C (375°F). Toss the potatoes in the oil in a roasting tin and roast for about 30 minutes; they should be slightly coloured and starting to dehydrate a little.

While the potatoes are roasting, mix the mint leaves, coriander, parsley and dill together with the onion. In a large bowl, whisk together the olive oil, lemon juice and za'atar and set aside.

In a small saucepan over a medium–high heat, warm 100 g (3½ oz) of the butter until it splits. Turn the heat up – it should start to foam and smell nutty. Using a whisk beat the melted butter until the milk solids caramelise. Carefully pour this out into a heatproof bowl and add one of the minced garlic cloves so it cooks a little. Set aside to cool. Once the mixture is room temperature, add the shredded mint. This awesome butter mix is for tossing the potatoes in.

Next heat up a large non-stick pan until very hot. Add a touch of oil, then the sweetbreads. Sear on both sides until golden, then add the remaining butter, garlic and the thyme. Season with ground black pepper and, using a spoon, baste the sweetbreads with this mixture a few times so it cooks evenly and the butter doesn't burn. The whole process should take about 5 minutes.

Remove the pan from the heat and let the sweetbreads cool. Once they are cooled, chop them and put them in a large bowl. Take the potatoes out of the oven and roughly break them up and mix with the garlic butter. Next add the potatoes to the bowl with the sweetbreads, mix and check the seasoning – it might need a bit of lemon juice. Put this mix on a warm platter. Dress the herb and onion salad with the za'atar, olive oil and lemon dressing and, using your hands, sprinkle it over the potatoes and sweetbreads to garnish.

Lamb 'Shawarma' with Slow-roasted Figs and Tahini

Ingredients

2 premium lamb rumps

flaked salt for seasoning

2 teaspoons ground cinnamon

1 teaspoon cardamom

1 tablespoon coriander seeds

1 tablespoon ground turmeric

30 g (1 oz) paprika

2 tablespoons cumin

2 teaspoons ground black pepper

6 figs

50 g (1¾ oz) butter

20 ml (1 oz) red-wine vinegar

1 tablespoon sugar

1 bunch kale, leaves roughly torn

100 g (3½ oz) tahini

juice of 2 lemons

Pickled red onion

1 red onion, cut into wedges
about 0.5 cm (1/2 in) thick
and broken into pieces

20 ml (¾ fl oz) grape seed oil

1 teaspoon sumac

50 ml (1¾ fl oz) white vinegar

50 g (1¾ oz) sugar

I call this 'shawarma' (marinated meat cooked on a rotisserie) but this recipe gives a modern-day spin to the classic – and magnificent – street snack. Premium lamb rump is pan-seared and roasted, then combined with the lush sweetness of slow-roasted figs and the earthiness of tahini. It's the perfect balance.

Method

In a non-stick frying pan on a medium–low heat, place the lamb rump skin side down. Sprinkle a nice amount of flaked salt over the lamb rump and cook for around 10 minutes, then flip over and cook on the underside for 1 minute, followed by searing the four other edges. Remove from the heat and rest the lamb. (It's very hard to over-rest meat; I would suggest a minimum of 20 minutes.)

Blend the spices in a spice grinder or a very dry blender, and set aside.

Preheat the oven to 160°C (320°F). Stand the figs up in a roasting tin. Add the butter, vinegar and sugar and roast in the oven for around 15 minutes. Halfway through the cooking time, baste the figs with the pan liquid.

To make the pickled red onion, in a saucepan over a high heat, combine all the ingredients with with 50 ml (1¾ fl oz) water. Bring it to a rapid boil then remove from the heat and let the onion cool to room temperature in the liquid.

In the same pan you cooked the lamb in, sauté the kale until it is crispy verging on burnt and season with some more flaked salt.

When the figs are done, take two of them and blitz in a blender with the tahini and lemon juice to make a fig tahini. Keep the oven on.

Once it's done resting, put the lamb in the oven for 5 minutes to warm up.

To serve, spread the fig tahini on the plate. Slice the lamb rump and lay it flat on the dish, and add the figs (if they are large, I would cut them down slightly). Dust the dish with the spice mix, garnish with the pickled red onion and kale and serve.

LEBANON

CAPITAL
Beirut

OFFICIAL LANGUAGE
Arabic

AREA
10,400 sq km

POPULATION
6,100,000

CURRENCY
Lebanese pound

Lebanese culture is hospitable, generous and family-driven, and commensality (the practice of eating together at the same table) is a fundamental part of it. (You'll be unlucky to leave a gathering without a foil-wrapped parcel of leftovers for later.)

Mezze in Lebanon is largely vegetable based, but lamb, fish, goat and chicken can also feature. In a typical spread with friends and extended family, there can be up to 30 mezze on the table. To finish, there's usually a strong, sweet brew of Lebanese coffee served in a tiny cup.

Mainstay mezze include tabouleh made from burghul (bulgur wheat) and loads of parsley, and flame-burnt eggplant (aubergine) smooshed into baba ghanoush to be scooped up with pitta. Expect a jar or two of homemade pickled veg, as is the way for cuisines based heavily on seasonality, along with creamy labne drizzled with virgin olive oil, and maybe a garlicky, crunchy fattoush (bread salad) laced with sumac.

In the fertile Beqaa Valley, prime growing country with its mild Mediterranean climate, there are fig and pomegranate orchards, along with century-old olive groves. Lebanese olive oil is some of the world's most highly prized, and friends and families will often gather for the harvest and pressing.

Za'atar, a spice mix of sumac, thyme and sesame seeds, is an essential Lebanese pantry staple to flavour meats, fish, salads, or as a topping for fresh rounds of Lebanese bread with a bit of olive oil.

AUTUMN

CORE INGREDIENTS

HERBS & SPICES
cardamom, cassia, cloves,
coriander seed, cumin, garlic,
mint, nutmeg, paprika,
parsley, pepper, sumac,
thyme, za'atar

NUTS & SEEDS
almonds, cashew nuts, pine
nuts, pistachio nuts, sesame
seeds, walnuts

VEGETABLES
carrot, cauliflower, cucumber,
eggplant (aubergine), green
beans, tomato

MEATS & SEAFOOD
chicken, fish, goat, lamb

FRUITS
date, fig, lemon, olives,
pomegranate

DAIRY & EGGS
labne, milk, yoghurt

GRAINS & LEGUMES
beans, burghul (bulgur
wheat), chickpeas, lentils

FATS & OILS
olive oil

SPECIALITY & OTHER
coffee, flatbread,
grape leaves, orange
blossom, pickled turnip,
rosewater, tahini

AUTUMN

Labne with Squeezed Tomato

Ingredients

1 kg (2 lb 3 oz) yoghurt

2 jalapeños

100 ml (3½ fl oz) best-quality olive oil

1 garlic bulb

zest of 1 lemon

juice of 3 lemons

4 very ripe tomatoes

4 large pitta breads

How fancy will you feel making your own labne? While you need to start it the day before, it is fun and super simple to achieve. Top-notch presentation takes this dip to next-level status, so make sure you get the swirl right, with an even distribution of flavour. Jalapeños pack a hot punch and are my preferred chilli to use for the oil. For a milder heat, use finger-length green chillies.

Method

The night before, line a strainer with muslin (cheesecloth). Scoop the yoghurt in and set the strainer over a large bowl to catch the liquid that drips out overnight. (This liquid can be used for other preparations like salad dressings, but for this recipe you just want the labne!)

Also the night before, finely dice and deseed the jalapeños and soak in the oil overnight.

The next day, preheat the oven to 200°C (400°F). Wrap the garlic bulb in foil and put it on a baking tray. Roast it in the oven for 25 minutes, then remove it from the oven and rest it until it's cool enough to handle. Once it's cool enough, squeeze the roasted garlic out of its skin.

Put the labne in a food processor, add the roasted garlic and season with salt. Process, then add in the lemon zest and juice. (I love acidic foods so I go hard, but feel free to reduce the lemon juice to your taste.)

Cut the tomatoes in half crossways, like you would with a lemon.

Using a spoon, pile all the labne in the middle of a plate. Put the tip of your spoon against the plate in the middle of the pile of labne and spin the plate while pulling the spoon closer to yourself to create a swirl. On one side of the swirl, spoon the jalapeños and the oil and on the other half squeeze the tomato like a lemon, so you just get the seeds and juice.

Toast the pitta in a toaster, then cut them up into quarters and serve. If the pittas are ready early, just wrap them in a clean tea towel (dish towel) so they stay soft and hot.

● VEGETARIAN

Broccoli Tabouleh with Stem

Ingredients

1 bunch coriander (cilantro), leaves picked

2 bunches parsley, leaves picked

2 bunches dill, fronds picked

1 garlic clove

juice of 1 lemon

½ teaspoon cardamom

2 tablespoons best-quality olive oil

2 heads of broccoli

150 g (5½ oz) burghul (bulgur wheat)

1 Lebanese (short) cucumber

50 g (1¾ oz) dill pickles

½ preserved lemon

1 teaspoon grape seed oil

2 leeks, white part only,
1 diced, 1 sliced very thinly into
a few rings using a mandoline,
the remainder diced

100 g (3½ oz) sunflower kernels

Tabouleh is one of my favourite salads for its filling, wholesome zestiness. This recipe uses the entire head of broccoli (stem and leaves, too), loads of herbs, and nutty sunflower kernels to create something green, mean and lean. It's as good-looking as it is nutritious!

Method

Put the coriander, one of the bunches of parsley and one of the bunches of dill in the blender. Add the garlic, lemon juice and cardamom and blend on high speed for around 30 seconds. Pour it out into a container and pour the olive oil on top, so that it splits. Set aside.

Using a grater, grate the green tops of the broccoli and set aside. Reserve the stem, halving it lengthways.

Half-fill a saucepan with water and add the burghul. Bring it to the boil and cook for about 10 minutes, then strain and spread it out on a flat tray so it doesn't overcook.

Dice the cucumber and the dill pickles. Finely dice the preserved lemon and mince the remaining herbs.

In a large, wide frying pan over a medium heat, warm the oil. Put the broccoli stem and diced leek in the frying pan, cut side down. Cook until the leek and broccoli stem have quite a lot of colour and are cooked through, around 10 minutes.

Combine the cucumber, pickles, preserved lemon and minced herbs in a large bowl with the broccoli 'tabouleh', the cooked burghul, diced leek and sunflower kernels. Dress with the herb purée and garnish with the leek rings and broccoli stem.

● VEGAN

Fattoush

Ingredients

3 stale pitta breads

150 g (5½ oz) butter

2 garlic cloves, unpeeled

1 tablespoon za'atar

4 small Lebanese (short) cucumbers, sliced

2 tomatoes, roughly diced

1 red onion, sliced and washed in ice-water then dried on paper towel (this removes the astringent flavour)

1 bunch parsley, picked and roughly chopped

1 bunch mint, picked and roughly chopped

2 medium to large cos (romaine) lettuces, halved lengthways

Sumac, garlic and feta vinaigrette

juice of 2 lemons

60 ml (2 fl oz/¼ cup) good-quality olive oil

1 teaspoon sumac

40 g (1½ oz) Danish feta

2 garlic cloves (reserved from the breadcrumbs)

I love this bread salad for its crunch and sour sumac tang. Source the best-quality sumac, with the aroma and glowing colour of fresh berries. The dressing works with lots of different veggies and greens, so don't feel locked in by these ingredients – experiment with your own spin on this Lebanese classic.

Method

First make the breadcrumbs by pulsing the pittas in a blender until it has a thick, crumb-like texture. In a large saucepan over a medium heat, melt the butter with the unpeeled garlic and the breadcrumbs. Once all the butter has melted, turn the heat up and whisk until the breadcrumbs are golden brown. Strain the breadcrumbs (the butter can be reserved for another dish). When cool enough to handle, take the garlic out of the breadcrumbs and squeeze it out of its skin into a blender. Season the crumbs with a pinch of salt and make sure they are crunchy and have an intense garlic flavour, then mix in the za'atar for colour and flavour.

For the vinaigrette, add all ingredients to the blender with the garlic and blend. It should be just thinner than mayonnaise consistency. Splash some vinaigrette on a serving plate.

Mix all the remaining salad ingredients but the cos lettuce in a large bowl and pour over the remaining vinaigrette. Using your hands, push the salad into the grooves of the cos so that it is stuffed with the salad. Crumble the breadcrumbs over and serve.

● VEGETARIAN

93

Za'atar Roasted Chicken with Fatteh

Ingredients

1 free-range butterflied chicken

40 ml (1¼ fl oz) grape seed oil

1 garlic clove, minced

1 tablespoon za'atar

250 g (9 oz) cooked chickpeas
(tinned is okay)

60 g (2 oz) tahini

chopped parsley to serve

pinch of aleppo pepper or paprika
for dusting

Fatteh

375 g (13 oz) yoghurt

½ teaspoon cumin

1 white onion, diced

½ bunch parsley, leaves picked

½ bunch dill, fronds picked

50 ml (1¾ fl oz) olive oil

2 teaspoons za'atar

1 teaspoon salt

2 teaspoons pomegranate molasses

40 g (1½ oz) toasted walnuts, chopped

Tangy, herby za'atar is queen of the spice blends in Lebanon, and every family has its own version. Here, I've used it as a rub for chicken, teaming it with fatteh to add a cooling, creamy element to the dish. Fatteh is a classic breakfast dish eaten in the Levantine, and the spiced yoghurt is also a delicious spread for stale flatbread. It uses a core Middle Eastern ingredient: pomegranate molasses, available from specialty grocers.

Method

Preheat the oven to 140°C (275°F). Rub the chicken with 20 ml (¾ fl oz) of the oil and the minced garlic, put in a roasting tin and roast for 50 minutes.

Remove from the oven and increase the temperature to 200°C (400°F). Mix the next 20 ml (¾ fl oz) of oil with the za'atar and a pinch of salt and pour over the chicken. Return to the oven and roast for 10 minutes.

Fold the chickpeas through the tahini and set aside.

To make the fatteh, combine all the ingredients in a large bowl, then transfer to a saucepan warm the fatteh very gently over a low heat; it's not meant to be to hot, just warm.

Spread the chickpea mix and the fatteh on opposite sides of a serving platter or wide shallow bowl. Place the chicken on the serving platter whole. Using a fine strainer, dust it with some aleppo pepper or paprika and serve.

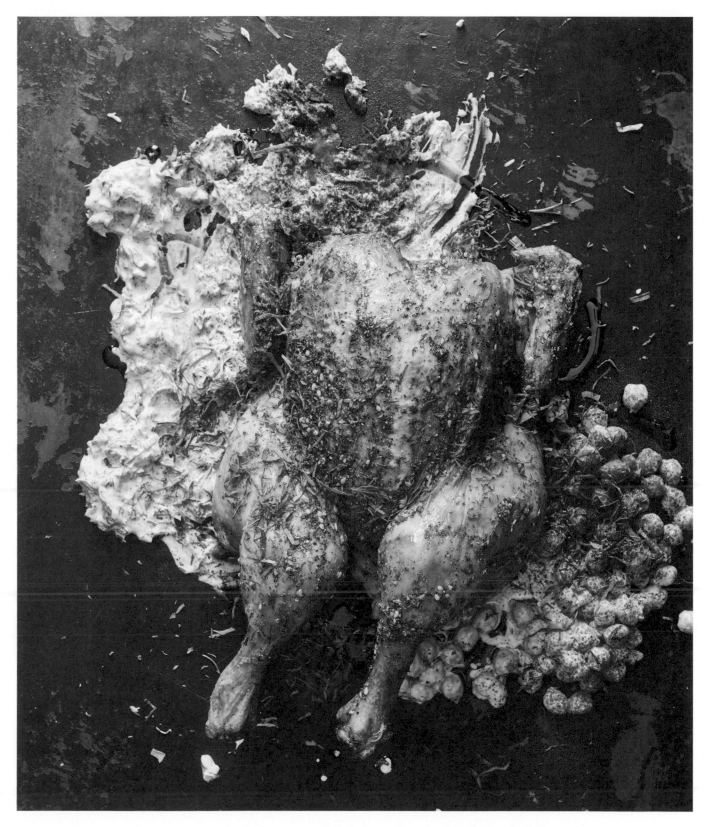

IRAQ

CAPITAL
Baghdad

OFFICIAL LANGUAGES
Arabic and Kurdish

AREA
438,320 sq km

POPULATION
40,194,220

CURRENCY
Iraqi dinar

Neighbours Iran, Turkey and Syria influence Iraqi food, but its biggest driver is religion, with a population that is 95 per cent Muslim. Its cuisine dates back a whopping 10,000 years to 8000 BC, with many culinary traditions and feasts based on religious ceremonies, such as Ramadan.

People eat in the way that is typical of most Middle Eastern countries: mezze, sharing lots of small dishes, such as salads, vegetables, dips and bread.

Dates, considered 'the holy fruit', are believed to have originated in Iraq, and Iraqi dates are considered the world's best. Until recently Iraq was the world's biggest producer of dates, growing more than 300 varieties, but crops have been devastated due to severe conflict so it's now in fourth position. National projects and mass-plantings of date palms are underway to revive the flagging industry, and dates are still a core ingredient of Iraqi cuisine, eaten plain, before dawn during Ramadan, and in stews and sweets.

Spice mixes are big in Iraqi kitchens, used when cooking rice, to sprinkle over the top of dishes as you would salt, or used as rubs for meats.

Advieh is a staple blend, a combo of cardamom, cinnamon, rose petals, pepper, turmeric and cloves, and amba is another favourite, comprising mustard seeds, cumin, fenugreek and ground turmeric for that rich yellow hue. You can buy spice blends ready-made from Middle Eastern grocers, or toast and grind the spices to make your own mix, which is very satisfying (and aromatic!) if you have the time.

CORE INGREDIENTS

HERBS & SPICES
advieh spice mix, baharat spice mix, cardamom, cinnamon, cloves, cumin, dill, fenugreek, mint, mustard seeds, saffron, sumac, turmeric

NUTS & SEEDS
almonds, pine nuts, pistachio nuts, sesame seeds, walnuts

VEGETABLES
eggplant (aubergine), okra, tomato, turnip, zucchini (courgette)

MEATS & SEAFOOD
beef, chicken, lamb

FRUITS
apple, apricot, date, dried lime, olives, pomegranate, quince, raisin

DAIRY & EGGS
feta, haloumi, yoghurt

GRAINS & LEGUMES
barley, burghul (bulgur wheat), chickpeas, rice

FATS & OILS
olive oil

SPECIALITY & OTHER
date syrup, halva, orange blossom water, pomegranate molasses, rosewater, tahini

AUTUMN

Baba Ghanoush with Mint Olive Oil and Savoury Halva

Ingredients

2 large eggplants (aubergines)

20 ml (¾ fl oz) grape seed oil

juice of 2 lemons

½ large garlic bulb, broken into cloves and peeled

150 g (5½ oz) tahini

50 ml (1¾ fl oz) extra virgin olive oil

1 teaspoon salt

1 tablespoon paprika

Mint olive oil

1 bunch mint, leaves picked

100 ml (3½ fl oz) olive oil

Savoury halva

100 g (3½ oz/⅔ cup) sesame seeds

50 g (1¾ oz/⅓ cup) almonds

60 g (2 oz) pitted dates, finely sliced

110 g (4 oz) tahini

A sweet Iraqi treat, halva is usually made from tahini and hot sugar syrup and cuts like a crumbly cake. With this recipe, I've used halva as a savoury element, counteracting the slight bitterness of the tahini with dates.

Method

Preheat the over to 180°C (350°F). To make the savoury halva, toast the sesame and the almonds separately in an oven – watch the sesame, as it burns quickly. You are just looking to bring a bit of life to the sesame and almonds. Set aside.

Increase the oven temperature to 200°C (400°F). Put the eggplants on a baking tray and roast for 20 minutes. Remove from the oven and raise the temperature to 230°C (445°F), then split the eggplants in half and place them back on the tray, skin side down. Brush them with a touch of grape seed oil and place back into the oven for another 20 minutes.

In a blender coarsely blitz the toasted almonds and sesame for the halva. Add in the dates and tahini and bring together on a low speed, but don't overwork it. It should be moist but crumbly, and if you press it between your hands it should stick to itself.

Using a sharp knife slice the mint into the thinnest, most hair-like strands possible and then marinate in the olive oil for at least 10 minutes.

When the eggplant has roasted, scoop the flesh out into a blender and blend with the remaining ingredients (except the paprika) until smooth.

To plate, spoon the baba ghanoush onto a plate and create a well in it. Drizzle the mint oil around the well and place the savoury halva inside. Dust with the paprika.

AUTUMN

● VEGAN

Raw Apple and Caramelised Walnuts with Advieh

Ingredients

1 white onion, diced

60 g (4½ oz) flatbread or wrap-style bread, torn into small pieces

110 ml (4 fl oz) olive oil

juice of 2 lemons

4 green apples (or whatever type of apple is most delicious in your opinion)

2 cucumbers, sliced very thinly

4 red witlof (endive), leaves separated

Advieh spice mix

1 tablespoon cardamom

25 g (1 oz) cumin

½ teaspoon ground cinnamon

½ teaspoon rose petals

½ teaspoon ground black pepper

¼ teaspoon ground turmeric

½ teaspoon cloves

Caramelised walnuts

75 g (2¾ oz) sugar

300 g (10½ oz) walnuts

1 teaspoon advieh spice mix

1 teaspoon pomegranate molasses (available from speciality grocers)

1 teaspoon cumin

● VEGAN

This nutty, sweet–tart vegetarian salad is inspired by dolma, where meat or spiced rice fillings are wrapped in grape or cabbage leaves. Instead of using vine leaves, I've used very thinly shaved apple, which adds crunch and sweetness. You can buy advieh spice mix, if you're short on time.

Method

To make the advieh spice mix, put everything in a blender and blitz to a fine mix. Put in an airtight container – you will have a lot more than you need for this recipe, but it's a handy mix to have on hand.

To make the caramelised walnuts put the sugar in a very clean large, wide saucepan and put it on the highest heat possible. Do not stir or shake the pan. If it starts to burn in any area much faster than the others, drip some water on those areas. Once the caramel is dark and just starts to give off some smoke, throw in half of the walnuts, a large pinch of the advieh spice mix, the pomegranate molasses and the cumin and quickly stir to combine. Pour into a cold heatproof bowl or baking tray and set aside to cool as quickly as possible. Don't play with caramel – it's hot!

Heat 60 ml (2 fl oz/¼ cup) of the olive oil in a saucepan over a medium–low heat and slowly sauté the remaining walnuts with the onion and bread for about 20 minutes – try not to colour anything. Remove from the heat and let it cool down in the pan. Once it's cool enough to handle, roughly mince the mixture and season with 20 ml (¾ fl oz) of the lemon juice and some salt.

Next slice the apple cheeks on a mandoline, place in a large bowl and dress with the walnut mince and a touch of lemon juice to soften the apples. Add the cucumber and the witlof leaves. Whisk together the remaining lemon juice and olive oil, pour it over the salad and mix to coat. Transfer to a serving dish and garnish with the caramelised walnuts.

Zucchini and Rocket Salad with Dried Fruits

Ingredients

2 heaped tablespoons finely chopped dried apricots

2 heaped tablespoons finely chopped dried prunes

2 heaped tablespoons finely chopped dried figs

40 g (1½ oz) finely chopped raisins

40 g (1½ oz) finely chopped pine nuts

1 teaspoon pomegranate molasses (available from specialty grocers)

drop of orange blossom water (if you don't have it, use the zest of an orange)

40 g (1½ oz) tahini

200 g (7 oz) rocket (arugula)

4 zucchini (courgettes), very thinly sliced

Dressing

50 ml (1¾ fl oz) grape seed oil

2 red capsicums (bell peppers), diced

2 shallots, diced

2 garlic cloves, minced

½ teaspoon cumin

½ teaspoon paprika

juice of 1–2 lemons, depending on their acidity

1 teaspoon pomegranate molasses

20 g (¾ oz) toasted pine nuts

2 tablespoons good-quality olive oil

● VEGETARIAN

When I make this recipe I like to make extra dressing. It's such an intense, flavour-packed sauce and is delicious on roasted meats and fish, as well as salads and veggies – pretty much anything! It's especially handy if you've got an excess of zucchini (courgettes) growing in your garden.

Method

To make the dressing, heat the oil in a frying pan over a low heat and sweat the capsicum, shallot and garlic. You don't want it to colour. Once the shallot is translucent add the cumin, paprika and 200 ml (7 fl oz) water, put the lid on and cook, still on a low heat, until the water has evaporated. Remove it from the heat and stir in the remaining ingredients.

In a bowl combine the dried fruits with the pine nuts, molasses, orange blossom water and tahini. Taste – it may need a pinch of salt, depending on the sweetness of the dried fruits.

Check the seasoning on the dressing. In a large bowl, coat the rocket and zucchini quite heavily with the dressing. Sprinkle over the dried fruit salad and serve.

Amba Rice Salad with Almond Feta

Ingredients

400 g (14 oz/2 cups) basmati rice

1 white onion, diced

2 garlic cloves, sliced

40 ml (1¼ fl oz) grape seed oil

1 teaspoon amba spice mix

40 g (1½ oz) pepitas (pumpkin seeds)

40 g (1½ oz) sultanas (golden raisins)

100 g (3½ oz) almond feta
(or regular feta)

100 g (3½ oz) almonds, roughly
chopped

Amba spice mix

3 tablespoons mustard seeds

2 tablespoons cumin

1 tablespoon ground black pepper

1/4 teaspoon ground coriander

1/4 teaspoon fenugreek seeds

25 g (1 oz) paprika

25 g (1 oz) ground turmeric

If you're time poor, pick up ready-made amba spice mix from a **Middle Eastern** supermarket or grocer. But if you can, it's fun to make your own. Toss in as many of the ground spices you have at hand, or throw in different ones and create something new. The only ingredient you can't do without is turmeric for its vivid yellow hue.

Method

If you are making the spice mix, toast everything in a large frying pan over a high heat until it's aromatic. Put the toasted spice mix ingredients in a spice grinder or very dry blender and blitz until fine, then season with a pinch each of sugar and salt and set aside.

Wash the rice in a strainer under cold water until the water runs clear to remove some of the starch. Next place the onion, garlic, oil, spice mix, 1.1 litres (37 fl oz) water and the rice into a rice cooker and let it work its magic. If you are not using a rice cooker, put the onion, garlic, oil, spice mix, water and rice into a large saucepan and bring to a boil. Put the lid on and simmer on a low heat for 15 minutes, then remove from the heat and let it sit, covered, for a further 5 minutes.

Once the rice is ready, fluff it up using a fork and stir through the pepitas and sultanas with a pinch of salt. Sprinkle over the almond feta and almonds to garnish.

● VEGAN

ISRAEL

CAPITAL
Jerusalem

OFFICIAL LANGUAGES
Hebrew and Arabic

AREA
20,770 sq km

POPULATION
8,424,900

CURRENCY
Israeli shekel

Israel became a nation in 1948, but its culinary roots go way back – as in Old Testament way back – and there are mentions of olives, figs, dates, pomegranates, wheat, barley and grapes from biblical times.

A raft of cultural influences, from North African and Middle Eastern neighbours to Jewish immigrants from Eastern Europe and Russia, make modern-day Israeli food impossible to pigeonhole.

Speaking of pigeon, yes, this gamey bird does appear on Israeli menus, and can be given the kosher stamp of approval. 'Kosher' refers to the slaughter of animals in a prescribed way, and the practice of keeping all meat and milk products completely separate, to the point of using different pots and pans.

Mainly, though, vegetables (pickled, stuffed with rice, or turned into amazing salads and dips) are the hero ingredients of Israeli cuisine and, for this reason, I've included three vegan recipes in this chapter.

Tahini, the delicious peanut butter–like paste made from hulled sesame seeds, is a vital pantry staple, adding authenticity to Israeli cooking. You'll need it to make my Signature hummus, a recipe I swore I'd never share but that I've included opposite as a bonus – what's Israeli food without hummus, after all?

Signature Hummus

On the streets of Jerusalem, at a stall open from 5 am to 10 am and run by a 15-year-old boy and his dad, I ate the best hummus of all time. It was mind-blowingly fresh, served hot, with white onion cut into 'spoons' for scooping, pickled cucumber and bread. My signature hummus is inspired by that experience, but has a heavier hand with the tahini. It's simple, cheap, comforting, and a must-have addition for any Israeli mezze.

CORE INGREDIENTS

HERBS & SPICES
amba spice mix, chives, cinnamon, coriander, cumin, dill, fenugreek, green chilli, mint, paprika, parsley, za'atar

NUTS & SEEDS
pistachio nuts, sesame seeds

VEGETABLES
artichoke, cabbage, carrot, cauliflower, cucumber, eggplant (aubergine), fennel, lettuce, onion, potato, tomato, zucchini (courgette)

MEATS & SEAFOOD
beef, chicken, fish, lamb, pidgeon, turkey

FRUITS
apple, avocado, banana, cherry, date, fig, grape, grapefruit, lemon, loquat, lychee, nectarine, olives, orange, persimmon, plum, pomegranate, pomelo, prickly pear, strawberry, tangerine

DAIRY & EGGS
egg, feta

GRAINS & LEGUMES
barley, rice, semolina, wheat

FATS & OILS
olive oil, *schmaltz* (rendered chicken or goose fat)

SPECIALITY & OTHER
pickled veg, tahini

Ingredients

400 g (14 oz) dried chickpeas

20 g (¾ oz) salt

20 g (¾ oz) cumin

375 g (13 oz) tahini

juice of 2 lemons

olive oil to garnish

● VEGAN

Method

Soak the chickpeas for a minimum of 4 hours. Drain, then put them in a large saucepan and cover with water. Boil for 1 hour and 45 minutes, or until tender. Fill a bowl with ice, then set another bowl on top.

Drain the chickpeas, reserving some to garnish, and add to a blender with all the remaining ingredients – except the lemon juice – and 600 ml (20½ fl oz) of fresh water. Blend until smooth. Pour it into the prepared bowl and whisk in the lemon juice. Garnish with the reserved chickpeas and olive oil.

Pickled Kohlrabi Mosaic with Burnt Fruits

Ingredients

1 large beetroot (beet), cut into 2.5 cm (1 in) dice

2 large red apples, cut into 2.5 cm (1 in) dice

2 large plums, cut into 2.5 cm (1 in) dice

1 kohlrabi cut into 2.5 cm (1 in) dice

60 ml (2 fl oz/¼ cup) red-wine vinegar

Pickled kohlrabi

50 ml (1¾ fl oz) good-quality white wine or chardonnay vinegar

50 g (1¾ oz) sugar

1 kohlrabi sliced as thinly as possible on a mandoline and

Herb dressing

250 ml (8½ fl oz/1 cup) good-quality olive oil

1 bunch parsley

½ bunch dill

½ teaspoon cardamom

½ teaspoon cumin

juice of 2 lemons

1 finger-length green chilli

● VEGAN

Art meets food with this visually stunning dish. Hot tip: if you've been thinking of buying a mandoline for your kitchen, now could be the time. Without one, it will be hard to achieve the thinness and neatness required for the mosaic presentation. Good luck, it's worth it!

Method

Put the beetroot in a medium saucepan and cove with water. Place over a high heat and boil for 10 minutes. Strain the beetroot and set aside to cool.

To make the pickled kohlrabi, boil the white-wine vinegar, sugar and 50 ml (1¾ fl oz) water together. Once it has boiled, add in the thinly sliced kohlrabi and remove from the heat and set aside.

To make the dressing, put 100 ml (3½ fl oz) of the olive oil in a blender along with the remaining ingredients and a large pinch of salt. Blend on a high speed for around 30 seconds. Pour it out into a container and pour the remaining olive oil on top – you want it to split.

Put a cast-iron pan or heavy-based saucepan over a high heat until it is very hot. Add a tiny amount of oil and wait until it smokes, then add in the boiled beetroot, the apple, plum and diced kohlrabi and reduce the heat to low. Cook until it is slightly blackened and then pour over the red-wine vinegar. Remove from the heat and put the fruits and vegetables in a large mixing bowl. Dress with the herb purée and mix to combine.

Place the mix on the plate and cover half the dish with the kohlrabi slices so the colours soak through and it looks like a mosaic.

Roasted Butternut with Red Onion and Pepitas

Ingredients

1 kg (2 lb 3 oz) butternut (squash) in a 3 cm (1¼ in) dice, skin on is fine

40 ml (1¼ fl oz) grape seed oil

pinch of salt

3 red onions, 2 quartered and 1 sliced into 1 cm (½ in) wide wedges

100 g (3½ oz) pepitas (pumpkin seeds)

1 teaspoon sumac

50 ml (1¾ fl oz) white vinegar

50 g (1¾ oz) sugar

1 teaspoon za'atar

Pepita tahini

120 g (4½ oz) pepitas (pumpkin seeds)

120 g (4½ oz) tahini

juice of 2 lemons

40 ml (1¼ fl oz) olive oil

I'm not going to lie: for a long time I thought butternut was a pumpkin. It tastes and looks a lot like one, but this vine-growing squash is typically sweeter and a brighter orange than its pumpkin doppelganger. For the dressing, I've mixed actual pumpkin seeds with tahini, which add a nutty depth to this moreish vegetarian winner. You can make or buy za'atar – but if you don't have any, you can always just crack some black pepper over the pepitas (pumpkin seeds) once toasted.

Method

Preheat the oven to 200°C (400°F) Line two baking trays with baking paper. Toss the diced butternut in a large bowl with a little bit of grape seed oil and a pinch of salt. On one tray put the butternut at one end, and the red onion quarters at the other. In a bowl combine the pepitas with half of the grape seed oil, then sprinkle them over the other prepared tray as flat as possible so they cook evenly. Put both trays in your oven. After 15 minutes the seeds will be ready – take them out and let them cool to room temperature. The butternut and onion mix will need a further 10 minutes.

In a saucepan over a high heat, combine the sliced red onion, the remaining grape seed oil, sumac, vinegar and sugar with 50 ml (1¾ fl oz) water. Bring it to a rapid boil then remove from the heat and let the onion cool to room temperature in the liquid.

For the pepita tahini, blitz all the ingredients and 105 ml (3½ fl oz) water at a high speed in the blender. Check the seasoning once it's puréed – it should be acidic and delicious.

To serve, spread the butternut and roasted onion over the plate and then pour over the pepita tahini in a wild fashion. Cover the dish with the vibrant pickled onion and sprinkle over the toasted pepitas.

AUTUMN

● VEGAN

Smoked Eggplant with Pistachio and Vine Leaves

Ingredients

½ garlic bulb, broken into cloves and peeled

juice of 4 lemons

135 g (5 oz/½ cup) tahini

pinch of cumin

300 g (10½ oz) pistachio nuts

3 large eggplants (aubergines)

2 tablespoons good-quality olive oil

8 fresh grape vine leaves

If you've ever wanted to cook like a qualified chef, now's your chance. At my Melbourne restaurant, I make this nutty, smoky, lemony eggplant (aubergine) dish exactly as it appears here. Don't worry, it's not too technical, and vine leaves are easy to source.

Method

Preheat the oven to 160°C (320°F).

Blitz together the garlic, half the lemon juice and a pinch of salt with a hand-held blender. Let it sit for 10 minutes. Pass it through a sieve, then add it to a blender with the tahini and cumin. Add 250 ml (8½ fl oz/1 cup) of cold water and mix furiously for a couple of minutes. Add 200 g (7 oz) of the pistachio nuts and blend until completely smooth. Season to taste with more lemon juice and salt and set aside.

Spread the remaining pistachio nuts on a baking tray and roast them for 8 minutes. Allow them to cool down and then using a mortar and pestle smash them into a nice crumble (or just chop them by hand) and set aside.

Using a gas stove or, even better, a charcoal barbeque, burn the skin of the eggplants until completely burnt on all sides, then halve them and scoop the flesh out into a bowl. Mix in the remaining lemon juice and olive oil and season to taste with salt. Try not to mash it too hard.

Place the seasoned eggplant on the plate, drizzle the pistachio tahini all over, then sprinkle over the crushed pistachios and garnish with the vine leaves.

● VEGAN

Knafeh

Ingredients

150 g (5½ oz) kataifi pastry

50 ml (1¾ oz) clarified butter

100 g (3½ oz) pistachio nuts

125 ml (4 fl oz/½ cup) milk

125 ml (4 fl oz/½ cup) cream

205 g (7 oz) sugar

3 eggs

250 g (9 oz) good-quality cheddar
cheese, grated

juice of 1 lemon

drop of rosewater or orange-blossom
water (if you don't have it, use the zest
of an orange)

Despite the focus of this book on savoury shareables, I couldn't resist including my knafeh. Semi-sweet but still savoury, syrupy, crunchy 'n' cheesy – it's crazily good. Adaptations of this Middle Eastern classic have been appearing since the tenth century and there are a myriad regional specialities, some with clotted cream, some with semolina. With this recipe you make your own cheese curd (it's simple, but don't turn your back!). Kataifi pastry is available from specialty grocers. When choosing pistachio nuts, look for the ones that are bright green.

Method

Preheat the oven to 165°C (330°F) and line a baking tray with baking paper. Brush the kataifi pastry with the clarified butter and then place on the baking paper in a large ring, about 8 cm (3¼ in) in diameter. Bake for 20 minutes or until golden, then remove from the oven and set aside. Spread the pistachio nuts on a baking tray and add them to the oven for about 6 minutes – you want to give them a slight colour and bring them back to life, but be careful not to burn them.

In a saucepan over a medium–high heat add the milk, cream, 15 g (½ oz) of the sugar, and eggs and whisk. Really watch it, as it can catch on the bottom of the pan and burn! Carefully add the cheese in slowly so it emulsifies. Once it has thickened slightly, strain it through a fine strainer and place in the fridge to cool down.

To make the sugar syrup, combine the remaining sugar with the lemon juice, rosewater and 2 tablespoons water in a saucepan over a high heat and boil it until it coats the back of a spoon, then remove from the heat and allow it to cool.

Place the cheese mixture into a piping (icing) bag and pipe into a bowl. (Alternatively, you can just spoon the cheese into the bowl.) Break the pastry in shards over the dish, then pour in the sugar syrup and sprinkle over the pistachio nuts and serve.

● VEGETARIAN

GREECE

PORTUGAL

WINTER

SPAIN

ITALY

FRANCE

GREECE

CAPITAL
Athens

OFFICIAL LANGUAGE
Greek

AREA
131,960 sq km

POPULATION
10,761,520

CURRENCY
euro

Greece's food culture is way more than nourishment. It's a deeply embedded way of life focusing on family, community, conviviality and lively conversation.

Influences on Greek cuisine come from its massive coastline spanning the Aegean, Ionian and Mediterranean seas, along with ingredients and dishes from the Ottoman Empire such as tzatziki.

Eat at a taverna for simply grilled seafood and meat and home-style bakes (such as moussaka rich with béchamel), often served with retsina (wine infused with pine-tree sap), or head to an ouzerie for a big spread of mezze and a couple of shots of ouzo (Greece's famous aniseed-flavoured spirit).

A typical Greek mezze might feature dolmades (grape leaves stuffed with rice and meat), zucchini (courgette) fritters, fava dip (made from yellow split peas), taramasalata (a dip made from fish eggs), meatballs, octopus, Greek salad, and, of course, pitta.

Pitta is a wheat-based, yeast-free flatbread, originating from Iraq during the Mesopotamian period. Many countries have their own take, but Greece's version is light and fluffy, perfect for wrapping charcoal-grilled meat to make an absolutely addictive souvlaki. Day-old pitta can be toasted and tossed in salads or dips.

Cheese fiends, Greece has an awesome cheese culture, particularly on the salty, sharp end of the flavour spectrum. Feta (made from sheep's or goat's milk) is a staple on all Greek tables, crumbled over salads, eaten fresh with a drizzle of olive oil, baked with spinach and puff pastry as flaky spanakopita, or wrapped in filo pastry and drizzled with honey. Kefalograviera and haloumi are floured and pan-fried to make saganaki.

Fossils of olive leaves and pollen have been found in Greece dating back to prehistoric times. In Athens, 'Plato's Olive Tree' was estimated to be 2400 years old, making it one of the world's oldest olive trees, before a bus knocked it over in 1976. Don't panic, there are still more than 160 million olive trees in Greece, the third-largest producer of olive oil in the world, and you'll find liberal use of quality olive oil in most dishes.

CORE INGREDIENTS

HERBS & SPICES
allspice, basil, bay leaf, clove, dill, garlic, mastic, mint, nutmeg, oregano, saffron, sumac, thyme

NUTS & SEEDS
almonds, walnuts

VEGETABLES
capsicum (bell pepper), caper, celery, eggplant (aubergine), fennel, Greek pepper, green beans, okra, onion, potato, tomato, zucchini (courgette)

MEATS & SEAFOOD
anchovy, beef, chicken, fish, lamb, octopus, pork, squid, veal

FRUITS
lemon, olives, orange

DAIRY & EGGS
cheese, egg, yoghurt

GRAINS & LEGUMES
lentils, pasta, white beans, yellow split peas

FATS & OILS
olive oil

SPECIALITY & OTHER
grape leaves, honey, ouzo

WINTER

119

Taramasalata with Black Olives and Pitta Bread

Ingredients

80 g (2¾ oz) pitted black olives, thinly sliced lengthways

40 g (1½ oz) olive oil

30 high-quality trout roe

4 large pitta breads

50 ml (1¾ fl oz) grape seed oil

Taramasalata

1 large pitta bread

150 g (5½ oz) fish roe

juice of 1 lemon

1 garlic clove

125 ml (4 fl oz/½ cup) olive oil

100 ml (3½ fl oz) vegetable oil

white pepper to taste

Taramasalata, one of the greatest gifts of Greek cuisine, is a must-have dish on most mezze. With fishy, garlicky and bright citrus flavours, and depth from toasted pitta bread, this classic dip is one of my faves. Traditionally, it's a coarse consistency, made using a mortar and pestle, but my recipe simplifies the process with a whiz in the blender. I guarantee this will be your new 'please bring a plate' go-to.

Method

To make the taramasalata, first char the pitta bread in a toaster. Break it into rough pieces and put it in a bowl, soak it in water until it's soggy, then strain off the water and set the bread aside. In a blender blitz the fish roe, lemon juice, and garlic to a purée, adding the pitta bread as needed to thicken. While the blender is running, slowly pour both the oils in until it forms a tasty mayonnaise consistency. Season to taste with white pepper and salt, keeping in mind that fish eggs are usually already quite salty.

Next, in a bowl combine the black olives, olive oil and trout roe. Brush the pittas with the grape seed oil, then toast in a toaster or under a grill (broiler) until golden and cut into wedges.

To serve, spread the taramasalata all over a serving plate and pour over the olive and trout roe mixture. Serve with the pittas on the side and you're ready for action.

Saganaki with Slow-cooked Onions

Ingredients

16 baby onions, peeled

60 ml (2 fl oz/¼ cup) premium red-wine vinegar

30 g (1 oz) sugar

40 g (1½ oz) butter

2 figs

2 bay leaves

200 g (7 oz) haloumi (or kefalograviera), cut into 4 pieces

flour for dusting

I absolutely love cheese. Salty kefalograviera and haloumi have high melting points, which means they can be pan-seared until golden brown on the outside and soft on the inside, while still keeping their overall shape. The most challenging part of this dish is not eating the whole block of cheese, especially when paired with this bittersweet mix of rich onion (good luck!).

Method

Preheat the oven to 145°C (295°F). Put the onions, red-wine vinegar, sugar, butter, figs and bay leaves in an ovenproof saucepan with a tight-fitting lid, and bake in the oven for 1.5 hours or until soft and broken down.

Once the onions are 10 minutes off, dust the saganaki pieces lightly with flour on both sides. Set a non-stick pan over a high heat and sear the saganaki pieces on both sides until golden.

Place the saganaki on the plate, then spoon over the slow-cooked onions and serve immediately.

● VEGETARIAN

Pickled Bonito, Capers and Potato Salad

Ingredients

400 g (14 oz) filleted bonito

200 ml (7 fl oz) oil for frying

70 g (2½ oz) capers, rinsed and
squeezed dry

Pickling liquid

150 ml (5 fl oz) white-wine vinegar

50 g (1¾ oz) sugar

1 teaspoon fennel seeds

30 ml (1 fl oz) ouzo (or another type
of aniseed liquor)

pinch of white pepper

1 garlic clove, minced

100 ml (3½ fl oz) olive oil

Potato salad

20 small waxy potatoes, boiled

10 g (¼ oz) dried oregano

juice of 2 lemons

50 ml (1¾ fl oz) olive oil

30 g (1 oz) pine nuts

Fancy some pickled fish but don't have a whole week to wait? Enter the quick pickle! This straightforward method of gently 'cooking' the bonito (available from Asian grocers) in a typical sugar-vinegar solution, then mixing in olive oil, gives a similar taste to the real thing but without the preservation properties. To make this dish vegan, substitute bonito with cucumber and follow the same method.

Method

First prepare the pickling liquid. In a saucepan bring all the ingredients except the olive oil to the boil. Pour in 150 ml (5 fl oz) water to cool the mix, then refrigerate.

Slice the fish into nice sashimi-sized pieces and set aside.

In a saucepan over a high heat bring the frying oil to 180°C (350°F), carefully drop the capers into the oil and quickly fry until there are no bubbles. That way they'll be nice and crisp. Using a slotted spoon, remove the capers from the oil and drain them on paper towel.

For the potato salad, with a large spoon roughly crush all the ingredients together in a bowl and set aside.

Take the pickling liquid out of the fridge and stir in the olive oil. Marinate the fish in the liquid for 5 minutes, which should slightly 'cook' the fish, and then remove it, reserving the liquid.

To serve, spoon the potatoes into the bowl. Using a spoon, place pieces of the fish in the gaps among the potatoes and then garnish with the capers. I would suggest using some of the pickling liquid to season the dish slightly further.

Winter Roasted Greek Salad

Ingredients

1 fennel bulb, cut into 8 wedges

1 red onion, quartered

100 ml (3½ fl oz) olive oil

pinch of salt

2 radicchios

4 celery stalks

juice of 1 lemon

50 g (1¾ oz/⅓ cup) pitted kalamata olives, halved

1 teaspoon dried oregano

100 g (3½ oz) almond feta

Who says Greek salad is only for summer? By using winter veggies, but keeping the same feta–oregano flavour profile, you can easily extend this salad's seasonality and eat it year-round. I love the combo of bitter leafy radicchio with the sharp, creamy cheese and fragrant, anise-like flavour of the fennel. Almond feta is a vegan nut cheese (sourced from speciality organic shops) – even if you're not vegan, it's a delicious swap in any dish requiring a soft white cheese.

Method

Preheat the oven to 200°C (400°F). Toss the fennel and onion together in a bowl with 30 ml (1 fl oz) of the olive oil and a pinch of salt. Put them in a roasting tin and roast them in the oven for 20 minutes.

Break the radicchio down into small leaves and slice the celery finely on a mandoline. You can do this lengthways along the spine of the celery and then soak the strips in ice-water to create curly celery. Then drain and toss the celery, radicchio and roasted vegetables together with the lemon, olives and remaining olive oil.

Plate up and garnish with the oregano and feta.

● VEGAN

PORTUGAL

CAPITAL
Lisbon

OFFICIAL LANGUAGES
Portuguese and Mirandese

AREA
92,090 sq km

POPULATION
10,355,490

CURRENCY
euro

WINTER

Portugal, on the tip of the Iberian Peninsula with Spain as its border, is a warm and generous country famed for its seafood. It's influenced by Mediterranean and Spanish cuisine, along with ingredients such as sugarcane and peri-peri, collected by Portuguese explorers when they set sail for Africa.

Peri-peri (Swahili for 'pepper-pepper') is a bird's eye chilli that grows wild in Africa. It's been found in Portuguese recipes since the fifteenth century as a fiery sauce with garlic, vinegar and paprika. Since then a myriad of recipes and regional incarnations have appeared (chilli, lemon and oil are the base ingredients), and it can be a hot sauce, spicy seasoning or marinade.

Sugarcane inspired a multitude of sweet, eggy pastry treats. The most well known is the Portuguese tart, a caramelised egg custard sprinkled with cinnamon, in pastry casing. Originally, monks in Lisbon made the tarts, before selling the recipe to the sugarcane refinery Pastéis de Belém in 1837; the same family still makes them using the original 'secret' recipe. It's one of my favourite desserts.

Living next door to the world's largest producer of olive oil means it's used liberally in Portuguese dishes – mild olive oil for cooking, and full-bodied, strongly flavoured olive oil for dipping bread or as salad dressing.

Learn to love bacalhau (salted cod) if you visit Portugal. There are 365 recipes for cooking cod, one for each day of the year ... so the story goes. It's caught in the icy waters off Norway and, in the days before refrigeration, fishermen would salt and dry the fish so it lasted the distance back home. It's a national food, and a stew of salted cod with potatoes, boiled eggs and olives is a typical dish, as are potato and salted cod deep-fried into fritters.

CORE INGREDIENTS

HERBS & SPICES
bay leaf, cinnamon, clove, cumin, garlic, nutmeg, oregano, parsley, paprika, pepper, star anise, turmeric, vanilla

NUTS & SEEDS
almonds

VEGETABLES
cabbage, carrot, kale, lettuce, mushroom, onion, peri-peri chilli, potato, tomato

MEATS & SEAFOOD
anchovy, beef, chicken, chorizo, clam, crab, fish, lobster, mussel, octopus, oyster, pork, salted cod, sardine, scallop

FRUITS
apricot, grape, lemon, melon, orange, pear, pomegranate, strawberry

DAIRY & EGGS
cheese, egg, yoghurt

GRAINS & LEGUMES
chickpeas, broad (fava) beans, rice

FATS & OILS
olive oil

SPECIALITY & OTHER
honey, madeira, quince paste, sugar

Grilled Bread with Slow-cooked Blood Orange, Anchovies and Black Olives

Ingredients

4 blood oranges

90 ml (3 fl oz) olive oil

20 ml (¾ fl oz) red-wine vinegar

4 garlic cloves, thinly sliced

4 slices of sourdough bread

12 high-quality, premium hand-filleted brown anchovies

100 g (3½ oz) pitted black olives, quartered

Juicy blood orange, intensely pungent anchovies and salty black olives make for a simple yet gutsy dish with briny, bittersweet flavours. It looks oh-so-casual, like you've just whipped it up, and it works a treat with a sour ale craft beer or mineral water with a lemon spritz.

Method

Preheat the oven to 125°C (255°F). Peel the blood oranges and cut them in half. Pour the oil and vinegar in a roasting tin, then put the blood oranges, cut side down, in the tin and cover them with the garlic. Roast in the oven for 1 hour or until the oranges have collapsed.

When you're ready to serve, toast the bread on a hot griddle to get some char marks. Place the blood orange, anchovies and olives in the middle of a serving plate with the bread to the side for your guests to build their own toast.

Bean Stew with Clams and Aïoli

Ingredients

250 g (9 oz) dried great northern
or white beans

100 ml (3½ fl oz) vegetable oil

1 onion, diced

200 g (7 oz) chorizo, diced

3 garlic cloves, minced

100 g (3½ oz) tomato paste

4 tomatoes, diced

1 teaspoon chilli flakes

1 teaspoon paprika

2 teaspoons salt

1 kg (2 lb 3 oz) clams (vongole)

120 ml (4 fl oz) white wine

Aïoli

1 garlic bulb

20 g (¾ oz) rock salt

2 egg yolks

2 teaspoons white-wine vinegar

200 ml (7 fl oz) grape seed oil

Comfort food at its best, this hearty and warming stew is chock-full of white beans, paprika-laced chorizo and fresh clams. If you like things spicy, use extra-hot chorizo and another shake of chilli flakes. Topping each bowl with aïoli adds creaminess and ties the whole dish together.

Method

Preheat the oven to 180°C (350°F).

In a bowl, cover the beans with lukewarm water and soak for a minimum of 1 hour.

For the aïoli, wrap the garlic bulb in foil and roast in the preheated oven for 30 minutes.

For the stew, warm the oil in a stockpot over a medium–high heat. Sauté the onion, chorizo and garlic until golden. Add the strained beans, tomato paste, tomato, chilli flakes, paprika and 1 litre (34 fl oz/4 cups) water. Bring to the boil, then reduce to a simmer. Let it simmer until the stew has thickened, then season with the salt.

Next make the aïoli. Squeeze the roasted garlic out of its skin and blitz in a blender with the salt, egg yolks and white-wine vinegar. With the motor running, slowly add the oil so that it emulsifies.

Put a large saucepan over a high heat. Once the saucepan is hot, add the clams, pour over the wine and cover the saucepan to steam them open. It may take up to 3 minutes until they are all opened. For any that don't open, stick a knife in and twist to shuck them. Pour the clams, with the stunning salty clam juice and wine, into the stew. Ladle into bowls for your guests and serve the aïoli on the side.

Romesco and Manchego Baked Potatoes

Ingredients

100 g (3½ oz) rock salt

12 medium roasting potatoes, skin on

150 g (5½ oz) manchego cheese, finely grated

Romesco sauce

2 red capsicums (bell peppers), whole

1 garlic clove

½ red onion, quartered

2 tablespoons grape seed oil

120 g (4½ oz) almonds, roughly chopped

60 g (2 oz) tomato paste

50 ml (1¾ fl oz) Pedro Ximenez vinegar or a nice red-wine vinegar

1 teaspoon paprika

½ teaspoon cayenne pepper

120 ml (4 fl oz) olive oil

● VEGETARIAN

Romesco (a Catalan sauce with tomato, capsicum/bell peppers and nuts as its core ingredients) and manchego (a sheep's milk cheese, often unpasteurised) are both originally from Spain, but they are common all over the Iberian Peninsula. In this recipe, they turn the humble spud into a baked potato of epic proportion.

Method

Preheat the oven to 180°C (350°F). Scatter a roasting tin with the salt, top with the whole potatoes and bake in the oven for approximately 40 minutes. They should semi-dehydrate and go crisp.

Meanwhile, for the romesco, add the capsicum, garlic and onion to a roasting tin, drizzle with the oil and toss to coat. Roast in the oven at the same time as the potatoes. Once the vegetables are roasted, approximately 25 minutes – they should be coloured and collapsed – remove and wait until they are cool enough to handle before roughly chopping, removing and discarding the seeds from the capsicum. Add the chopped vegetables to a blender with remaining romesco ingredients, then blitz into a thick sauce. Taste and adjust seasoning.

Once the potatoes are roasted, cut them into halves, leaving the skin intact. Carefully remove the flesh and in a bowl mix the romesco through the potato, then place the mixture back in the potato skins. Liberally scatter the manchego cheese on top and serve.

PORTUGAL

135

Grilled Octopus with Garlic and Rosemary

Ingredients

4 large octopus tentacles

2 garlic bulbs

2 bay leaves

1 teaspoon peppercorns

1 bunch rosemary

20 ml (¾ fl oz) grape seed oil

1 teaspoon paprika

50 ml (1¾ fl oz) vegetable oil

50 ml (1¾ fl oz) white-wine vinegar

Octopus is like squid: cook it super fast or let it simmer for hours; anything in between gives it an off-putting rubbery texture. But don't be scared of octopus either. I love it in salads, stews, or on its own as a snacky something-to-share with a glass of wine. In this recipe, the garlic and rosemary topping makes an amazing aromatic garnish, while the paprika adds pepperiness and colour.

Method

Bring a large saucepan of water to the boil and fill a large bowl with ice-water. Blanch the octopus tentacles in the boiling water for 3 minutes, then remove with tongs and submerge in the ice-water for 2 minutes. This process washes and tenderises the octopus. Repeat this process with fresh ice-water three times.

Put the octopus in a stockpot filled with water. Cut one of the garlic bulbs in half, then add both halves to the pot along with the bay leaves and peppercorns. Bring this to a simmer and cook for 1.5 to 2 hours. To test the tenderness, pull out a tentacle and cut a small piece off; it should be soft and delicate, not chewy.

While the octopus is cooking, preheat the oven to 180°C (350°F). Break the remaining garlic bulb up into cloves, then roast on a baking tray for 25 minutes. Remove the tray from the oven, scatter over the rosemary, drizzle over the grape seed oil and sprinkle with the paprika. Return to the oven and roast for a further 7 minutes until the rosemary is crisp and extremely aromatic.

Once the octopus is ready, pour out most of the water (but make sure the octopus is still covered), drop in a few ice cubes and let cool to room temperature. Remove the octopus from the liquid, put in a large bowl and pour over the vegetable oil and the white-wine vinegar. It can stay in the marinade for a maximum of 5 minutes – more than that and the vinegar will cook the octopus.

Remove the octopus from the marinade and place it all in spirals in a large non-stick pan with a touch of the marinade. Cook over a high heat, letting all the vinegar cook off. When the octopus is golden on one side, then flip and repeat on the other side. Plate it up and cover with a scattering of the garlic cloves and the rosemary!

SPAIN

CAPITAL
Madrid

OFFICIAL LANGUAGE
Spanish

AREA
505,370 sq km

POPULATION
49,331,080

CURRENCY
euro

Old meets new in Spanish cuisine, with recipes from indigenous clans, conquerors and explorers. The Celts, Iberians and Tartessians; the Romans, Greeks and Visigoths; the Arabs and the Europeans: all brought important ingredients, such as tomatoes, corn, chillies and potatoes, from the New World of the Americas, forever changing Spain's culinary evolution.

The country's food history is long and rich, but Spain also leads the world in contemporary dining, with many of its restaurants ranking highly in the acclaimed World's 50 Best Restaurants awards.

It's the largest producer of olive oil, with a tradition that goes back nearly 3000 years, and now provides nearly half the world's supply. The stable, southern Mediterranean climate in Andalucía makes it prime growing country, but different types of olive trees (introduced by modern-day Syria and Lebanon) thrive elsewhere and groves are found throughout the country. Spanish olive oil is fruity and nutty and a splash, drizzle or swirl is used to zhuzh most dishes.

Jamon is another star of Spanish cuisine. This intense, densely flavoured ham comes from black pigs allowed to roam the groves on the Iberian Peninsula, snuffling acorns, olives and chestnuts. Jamon is juicy and succulent, sliced thin, and served everywhere in Spain.

Lunch, from about 2 pm to 3.30 pm, is the main meal of the day, involving a multi-course affair if eating out, or at least a bowl of pasta or a stew if eating at home. Then it's siesta time, when many of the shops and restaurants close. Something snacky and small might be eaten at about 6 pm before the restaurants reopen at 9 pm-ish for dinner.

Rustic *tabernas* serve tapas (small plates) along with main-sized *raciones*, whereas *tascas* are bar-like spots where the drinks and small plates flow: things like gazpacho in a jug at the counter, a wedge of tortilla (which in Spain is like a frittata), marinated oil-slicked olives, fried baby squid, tomato-y meatballs, salt-cod croquettes, cheese, skewered meats, *patatas bravas* (fried potatoes) – you get the vibe! The food in Spain is some of the best you'll find in Europe.

CORE INGREDIENTS

HERBS & SPICES
aniseed, basil, bay leaf, cinnamon, garlic, paprika, rosemary, spearmint, thyme

NUTS & SEEDS
almonds

VEGETABLES
asparagus, cabbage, capsicum (bell pepper), carrot, celery, chard, corn, cucumber, mushroom, onion, peas, potato, spinach, tomato

MEATS & SEAFOOD
Iberian ham, lamb, pork, salted fish, squid

FRUITS
apple, cherry, fig, lemon, olives, orange, peach, pear, plum, quince, raisin

DAIRY & EGGS
cheese, egg, yoghurt

GRAINS & LEGUMES
broad (fava) beans, chickpeas, rice, white beans

FATS & OILS
olive oil

SPECIALITY & OTHER
honey, sherry, vinegar

WINTER

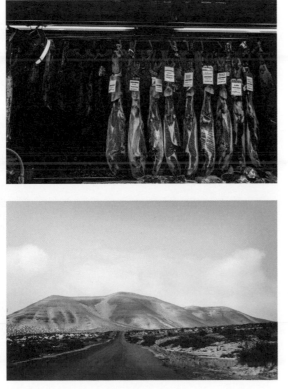

Green Gazpacho
with Thyme-pickled Mussels

Ingredients

2 green apples, peeled and roughly chopped

200 g (7 oz) ice

150 g (5½ oz) sourdough bread

½ white onion, roughly chopped

2 small cucumbers, roughly chopped

2 green capsicums (bell peppers), roughly chopped

2 celery stalks, roughly chopped

½ fennel bulb, roughly chopped

2 tablespoons white-wine vinegar

100 ml (3½ fl oz) good-quality olive oil

½ teaspoon sugar

½ teaspoon chilli flakes

3 garlic cloves

⅓ bunch coriander (cilantro), roughly chopped

⅓ bunch parsley, roughly chopped

⅓ bunch oregano, roughly chopped

4 slices high-quality bread

Thyme-pickled mussels

1 kg (2 lb 3 oz) mussels

100 ml (3½ fl oz) good-quality white wine

50 ml (1¾ fl oz) white-wine vinegar

50 g (1¾ oz) sugar

½ bunch thyme, leaves picked

2 garlic cloves, thinly sliced

1 white onion, cut into wedges about 0.5 cm (¼ inch) thick and broken into pieces

What makes a 'gazpacho' is the use of bread, olive oil, vinegar, water and salt; other than that, it's an open playing field. Gazpacho can be white, maybe with fresh or dried fig; it can be garlicky and red, with tomato; or bright green, as it is here, with a bunch of herbs and vegetables. And – get this! – it can also be served cold or warm. I've gone for warm here.

Method

In a blender blitz the apple with the ice. Line a strainer with muslin (cheesecloth) and place over a bowl to catch the liquid. Pour the blitzed apples into the muslin, then suspend the mixture over the strainer. It will take 1 hour for enough liquid to gather in the bowl. You will need 400 ml (13½ fl oz) of clear apple water.

When you're ready to make the gazpacho, soak the sourdough bread in 100 ml (3½ fl oz) of the apple water and set aside. Blitz the remaining apple water, all the vegetables, vinegar, 50 ml (1¾ fl oz) of the olive oil, sugar, chilli flakes and 2 of the garlic cloves in a blender; it should be quite thin. Throw in the herbs to get the maximum colour, blitz briefly, then add the soaked bread to thicken the dish and blitz again. Season with salt to taste and set aside in the refrigerator in a pouring jug.

Put a large saucepan over a high heat, then throw the mussels in and pour over the white wine. Cover with a lid and cook for about 1 minute, until they open. Remove from the heat and let it cool down before removing the mussels from their shells, checking them individually for beards (the clump of fibres that might still be attached to the mussels – they should be easy to cut off). In a small saucepan bring the vinegar, sugar, thyme leaves and garlic to the boil then pour it into a bowl with the onion. Once the onion has gone slightly limp, add in the mussels to cool it down. The mussels can stay in the pickling juice anywhere from 5 minutes to 2 hours.

Just before serving, brush the slices of bread with a touch of the remaining oil, then char on a hot griddle on each side until it is a little burnt. Using the bread as if it was a grater, rub the remaining garlic clove on the bread.

Pour the gazpacho into a saucepan and whisk over a medium heat. Warm to around 70°C (160°F) or to the point where it is just hot to the touch, then pour into the bowls. Spoon the mussels and the onion into bowls and pour over a dash of olive oil for freshness. Present the bread on a plate to the side.

Hot Brussels Sprouts with Mashed Potato and Poached Eggs

Ingredients

200 g (7 oz) rock salt

700 g (1 lb 9 oz) roasting potatoes, whole

500 g (1 lb 2 oz) brussels sprouts

200 ml (7 fl oz) milk

250 g (9 oz) butter

20 ml (¾ oz) grape seed oil

2 tablespoons vinegar

4 eggs

juice of 1 lemon

Sofrito

2 tablespoons grape seed oil

4 red capsicums (bell peppers), diced

2 garlic cloves, minced

2 brown onions, diced

1 teaspoon paprika

1 teaspoon cumin

The combination of sprouts, mash and poached eggs might sound French, because it is, but incorporating a sofrito (a Spanish pepper sauce) into this dish in a fusion of two cuisines creates something different altogether. Bake the potatoes before mashing them for a smoky flavour boost and, just like most French dishes, keep adding butter until you run out!

Method

Preheat the oven to 160°C (320°F). Scatter the salt on a baking tray, top with the potatoes and roast in the oven for 50 minutes.

To prepare the brussels sprouts, cut the core out of each with a small sharp knife and break each sprout up into separate leaves. Set aside.

For the sofrito, in a non-stick pan over a low heat, add the oil and cook the capsicum, garlic and onion, stirring occasionally, for about 35 minutes. The idea here is not to get colour, but to soften the vegetables. Once soft, mix in the paprika and cumin to create a vibrant red glow. Keep it warm over a very low heat.

When the potatoes are nearly done roasting, in a large saucepan gently warm the milk and butter.

Remove from the heat. Remove the potatoes from the oven and, while still hot, remove the skin by putting the potato in a clean tea towel (dish towel) in one hand and peeling the skin off with a small knife. Force the potatoes through a potato ricer. Add the potatoes to the warmed milk and whisk; it should be runny. Mash this mixture together as best as possible, then pass through a strainer to make sure it's smooth. Season with salt and return to the saucepan and cover. You can keep it over a very low heat so it stays hot, but if you work reasonably quickly it will stay hot if you just cover it.

Get a cast-iron pan, wok or griddle extremely hot, add the oil and quickly cook the brussels sprout leaves, trying to burn the edges, then set aside on paper towel.

Bring a large saucepan of water to the boil with the vinegar, then crack the eggs in and lower to a simmer for 3 minutes. Remove the eggs with a slotted spoon and set aside.

To serve, put a generous dollop of hot mashed potato on the plate and place the egg in the middle. Toss the brussels sprouts in the sofrito and put to the side. Let the yolk crack and run for colour, squeeze the lemon juice over it and enjoy.

WINTER

● VEGETARIAN

Seared Tuna on Warm Green Rice

Ingredients

100 g (3½ oz) pepitas (pumpkin seeds)

20 ml (¾ fl oz) grape seed oil

400 g (14 oz) tuna loin

50 g (1¾ oz) dijon mustard

olive oil to garnish

Green rice

2 tablespoons grape seed oil

80 g (2¾ oz) onion, finely diced

2 garlic cloves, finely diced

100 g (3½ oz) fennel, diced,
fronds reserved

400 g (14 oz) arborio rice

2 tablespoons pepitas
(pumpkin seeds)

2 teaspoons salt

1 bunch parsley

100 g (3½ oz) spinach

juice of 1 lemon

2 tablespoons butter

Rubbing mustard on a quality cut of tuna enhances its flavour, while searing it in a hot pan gives it a semi-crust – it's such a simple technique but one that adds real character and texture to the fish. Equally simple is the green rice, which has such a vivid colour and is packed full of nutrients. Toasty pepitas add the crunch.

Method

Preheat the oven to 170°C (340°F).

To make the green rice, heat the oil in a large saucepan over a medium heat and sauté the onion, garlic and fennel. Add the rice, pepitas, salt and 950 ml (32 fl oz) water and then stir and cook a bit like a risotto.

While this is cooking, fill a bowl with ice-water and place another bowl on top. In a blender blitz the parsley with the spinach and 150 ml (5 fl oz) hot water to create a loose purée. Pour it into the prepared bowl and whisk over the ice-water to cool it down immediately. Set aside.

Toss the pepitas in the oil, then spread them on a baking sheet and toast in the oven for 10 to 12 minutes.

Rub the tuna loin with the mustard and sear it quickly for about 30 seconds on each side in a hot non-stick pan (or on a piece of baking paper in a normal frying pan). Remove from the heat and carefully slice it (it should be very raw).

Season the rice to taste with more salt and the lemon juice and butter, then fold through the green purée. To serve, mound the green rice on the plate (it should be runny), top with the tuna slices and then garnish with a sprinkle of the toasted pepitas, reserved fennel fronds and a drizzle of olive oil.

Grilled Sardines in a Slow-braised Sauce

Ingredients

100 ml (3½ fl oz) olive oil, plus extra for brushing

4 red capsicums (bell peppers), diced

2 onions, diced

2 leeks, white part only, 1 diced, 1 sliced very thinly into rings using a mandoline, the remainder diced

3 garlic cloves, finely diced

2 bay leaves

1 cinnamon stick

300 g (10½ oz) tinned diced tomatoes

40 ml (1¼ fl oz) red-wine vinegar

30 g (1 oz) capers, rinsed and squeezed dry

½ teaspoon nutmeg

½ teaspoon paprika

12 fresh sardines (or anchovies), butterflied or filleted by your fish supplier

1 bunch parsley, leaves picked

Love them or hate them, sardines can divide a room. I adore them but if you don't, substitute a piece of white-fleshed fish, taking care not to overcook it, or you'll lose the 'fleshy' texture the white sardines bring to the dish. The fishy flavours work brilliantly with the typical Spanish spicing in the sauce.

Method

In a saucepan over a low heat, slowly simmer the olive oil, capsicum, onion, diced leek, garlic, bay leaves and cinnamon stick. You don't want it to colour or caramelise, so really take your time. Once the onions are translucent add in the tinned tomatoes, red-wine vinegar, capers, nutmeg and paprika and cook on a medium–low heat until the oil splits and it glows with that stunning vibrant red paprika colour. Remove the bay leaves and cinnamon, then set aside.

Next brush the sardines with a touch of oil and cook on a hot griddle, skin side down. It shouldn't take long, as they are such thin fish. Reheat the sauce and place on the plate. Put the fish on top of the sauce, and garnish with the picked parsley and leek rings.

ITALY

CAPITAL
Rome

OFFICIAL LANGUAGE
Italian

AREA
301,340 sq km

POPULATION
62,246,670

CURRENCY
euro

Who created pasta? Was it the Chinese, ancient Greeks, Sicilians? Was it the Etruscans, indigenous Italians who hail from Tuscany? The story of Marco Polo introducing pasta to Italy in the thirteenth century is a hoax, and, though it's impossible to know for sure, it's most likely Arabs are the original makers – and they're also credited with bringing dried pasta to Italy.

Today there's no question: Italians are the world's pasta masters, with over 300 forms of the simple wheat-flour–water combo, from fusilli to farfalle. It's eaten fresh, dried, sometimes with egg (such as wide, flat ribbons of pappardelle), and it's eaten often: in soups, salads, as first course, as a main, with seafood, with meat, with chilli, with bacon, with potato, with chocolate, with strawberry. Recipes are handed down through the generations with secret family recipes and techniques and every nonna making 'the best'.

Food changes within each Italian region, from the rugged Alps to the coastal Mediterranean to the fertile slopes of Tuscany, and there is real pride in these regional differences.

Calabria, with its Spanish influence, cooks with goat, pork and seafood, and loves chilli and spice, such as 'nduja (the spreadable chilli-pork salumi). In Abruzzo, you'll find wild mushroom dishes and lamb. The Emilia-Romagna region produces the famed Parmigiano Reggiano cheese, egg pastas and filled pastas, such as tortellini. There are so many regions, each one with its own historical connection and culinary customs, all of them quintessentially Italian.

Risotto, made with short-grain arborio rice and a hefty whack of butter, is another big player in Italian cuisine. It can be simple, with lemon as the only flavour, or dense with mushrooms, and it's usually eaten at the start of a meal.

Italy is the world's second-largest producer of olive oil, and the distinctive olive trees, with their grey-green leaves, are a common sight.

For this chapter, I collaborated with Bella Grand, my 'nearly sister-in-law'. With her Italian heritage and passion for the cuisine, she's a nonna in training.

CORE INGREDIENTS

HERBS & SPICES
basil, dill, garlic, parsley, rosemary

NUTS & SEEDS
chestnuts, pine nuts

VEGETABLES
artichoke, asparagus, capsicum (bell pepper), eggplant (aubergine), onion, porcini mushroom, radicchio, tomato, zucchini (courgette)

MEATS & SEAFOOD
anchovy, beef, chicken, fish, goat, lamb, lobster, pork, prawn, squid, swordfish

FRUITS
lemon, olives, watermelon

DAIRY & EGGS
cheese (particularly parmesan and ricotta), egg, milk

GRAINS, PASTA & LEGUMES
egg pasta, polenta, rice, wheat pasta, white beans

FATS & OILS
butter, olive oil

SPECIALITY & OTHER
balsamic vinegar

WINTER

Roasted Fennel and Goat's Cheese Bruschetta

Ingredients

2 fennel bulbs, cut into sixths

1 red onion, finely chopped

3 garlic cloves

1 handful basil, chopped, plus extra
to garnish

20 ml (¾ fl oz) grape seed oil

50 ml (1¾ fl oz) good-quality olive oil,
plus extra for brushing

1 good-quality baguette or loaf
of ciabatta bread, sliced

150 g (5½ oz) goat's cheese in oil
to serve

2 tablespoons balsamic glaze

Bruschetta is always a fast mover: who's going to argue with toasty garlic-rubbed bread laced with salt and olive oil? It's been a winning combo since the sixteenth century. I love this topping of roasted fennel and basil, but get creative with your own combinations. Oh, and if you're wondering how it's pronounced (who isn't?), Italians say 'bru-*sket*-uh', not 'bru-*shet*-uh'.

WINTER

Method

Preheat the oven to 190°C (375°F). Combine the fennel, onion, 2 garlic cloves and basil in a large mixing bowl and season to taste with salt. Drizzle over the grape seed oil and then roast on a baking tray for 20 minutes.

Lightly oil the bread slices using a brush. Toast the bread on a pan or sandwich press to your desired crispness. Then, using the bread as if it was a grater, rub the remaining garlic clove on the bread.

To serve, generously smear the goat's cheese on the bread. In a large mixing bowl, toss together the vegetables with the olive oil and place on top of the bread. Drizzle over the balsamic glaze, garnish with the basil and dig in!

● VEGETARIAN

Whole Burnt Cabbage Inspired by Vitello Tonnato

Ingredients

1 medium white cabbage

4 hard-boiled eggs

190 g (6½ oz) tinned highest-quality tuna in oil, drained

50 g (1¾ oz) tinned highest-quality anchovies in oil, drained

50 g (1¾ oz) capers, rinsed and squeezed dry

juice of ½ lemon

⅓ bunch parsley, leaves picked

Here, cabbage is given the rock-star treatment, transformed into a luxe dish that will have pescetarians raving. It's all about the texture of the caramelised cabbage and the umami-bomb hit of tuna and anchovies from the classic mayo-style Piedmontese sauce. You'll never look at cabbage the same way again.

Method

Preheat the oven to 200°C (400°F) and place the cabbage, whole, on a baking tray and roast for 1 hour. The idea is to burn it and let it caramelise.

Cut the eggs in half and carefully remove the yolks. (The whites can be reserved and eaten with some of the tuna sauce – it's delicious!) Add the tuna, anchovies, egg yolks and half the capers to a blender. Add the lemon juice and blend. Continue to add water until the consistency is smooth, but not too runny. Taste and perhaps add some extra lemon or capers, depending on desired flavour, and season with salt and pepper to taste

Dress tge parsley leaves in a dash of olive oil and a little extra lemon juice.

Place the cabbage on a serving plate and cut it to open the cabbage up. Put the sauce on the side and scatter the remaining capers on it. Garnish the cabbage with parsley to serve.

● VEGETARIAN

A Simple Risotto

Ingredients

30 ml (1 fl oz) good-quality olive oil

50 g (1¾ oz) butter

2 garlic cloves, chopped

1 white onion, diced

1 celery stalk, diced

500 g (1 lb 2 oz) arborio rice

250 ml (8½ fl oz/1 cup) white cooking wine

110 g (4 oz) pecorino, grated, plus extra to garnish

110 g (4 oz) parmesan, grated, plus extra to garnish

zest of 1 lemon

⅓ bunch dill to serve

Stock

2 celery stalks

1 carrot, chopped

1 white onion, chopped

¼ bunch thyme

Creamy, buttery and cheesy – risotto is one of those comfort dishes many people include in their 'top 10 dishes to master' list. I've included this minimalist version, with its lemony pecorino kick and home-made stock (so much better than anything you can buy). It's delicious paired with other dishes or eaten by itself. Once you've got this basic recipe down, go crazy! Add mushrooms, seafood, chicken, veggies, whatever you like.

Method

To make the stock, put all the ingredients in a stockpot with 4 litres (135 fl oz/16 cups) water and bring to the boil. Simmer for 2 hours, then strain, discarding the solids, and set aside.

In a large frying pan over a low heat, sauté the oil, butter and garlic. Allow the garlic to infuse the oil. Once the pan starts to heat up add the onion, stirring regularly. Once the onion is translucent, add the celery and stir. Once these have combined and softened, raise the heat to medium and add the rice and stir, ensuring all the rice is coated by oil before adding any liquid. Add the white wine and stir, allowing it to be almost completely absorbed. Add a ladle-full of stock, constantly stirring. It's important to avoid any rice sticking to the bottom of the pan. Make sure the stock is absorbed before adding the next ladle.

After about 30 minutes of adding stock and allowing it to absorb, taste to check the consistency of the rice. If it is still slightly undercooked, add more stock; if it is almost ready, add in pecorino and parmesan and stir through. At the last moment add one more small ladle of stock and the lemon zest and stir through. Season to taste, then let the risotto just spread itself out as you ladle it onto the warmed plate, and garnish with more of the grated cheese and the dill.

● VEGETARIAN

Ligurian Snapper Roast with Pumpkin and Sage Brown Butter

Ingredients

½ pumpkin (squash), cut into slices
1 cm (½ in) thick

olive oil, for roasting

10 pitted black olives

2 garlic cloves, halved

½ bunch sage, leaves picked,
roughly chopped

2 × 400 g (14 oz) whole snapper
(or another white fish of preference)

100 g (3½ oz) butter

⅓ bunch parsley, leaves picked,
roughly chopped

⅓ bunch dill, roughly chopped

Australia loves a roast, but if you're sick of reaching for the lamb leg, try this lighter-style seafood option. It is still wintry and warming, and works as part of a bigger spread, or is a great midweek option. I like to use small and sweet ligurian olives, grown in northern Italy; their fruitiness pairs well with the pumpkin and earthy sage-infused butter.

Method

Preheat the oven to 180°C (350°F) and line a baking tray with baking paper. In a large bowl combine the pumpkin and some olive oil, then spread out evenly on the prepared baking tray and roast for 20 minutes.

After 20 minutes add the olives and garlic with half of the sage and season with salt, pepper and more olive oil. Create a gap in the centre of the tray and put the snapper in the centre. Bake for 15 minutes.

While the fish is cooking, heat the butter in a small saucepan over a high heat and whisk until it foams and smells nutty, then throw in the remaining sage, remove from the heat and set aside.

When the fish is done cooking, serve it immediately on the pumpkin and garnished with the parsley, dill and sage brown butter sauce.

FRANCE

CAPITAL
Paris

OFFICIAL LANGUAGE
French

AREA
643,800 sq km

POPULATION
67,364,360

CURRENCY
euro

Charles de Gaulle said it all: 'How can you govern a country that has 246 varieties of cheese?'

France gave us *Guide Michelin*, steak frites and béarnaise sauce, cheesy croque monsieur, duck confit, mirepoix (that dish-defining base of onion, celery and carrot used the world over), haricot bean cassoulet, and a host of ingredients and flavours incorporated daily into food around the globe. So important is French cuisine that its 'Intangible Cultural Heritage' is recognised by UNESCO.

France has thousands of artisanal and regional variations of cheese. The top producers are accredited, labelled Appellation d'Origine Protégée (AOP), a prestigious standard marking its quality and origin. Comté is the most famous example of an AOC cheese, made with unpasteurised milk from cows that graze in the mountainous Jura region of eastern France.

French butter is the world's best, with 84 per cent minimum fat content, meaning it keeps its shape and is rich with butterfat. It is prime for brushing on layers of pastry to make croissants, for creating buttery tarragon sauce, or just for smearing on a baguette.

Bread is so much more than a crusty roll; it's a lesson in French history. From the sixteenth to the nineteenth centuries peasants subsisted largely on bread (hearty loaves made with buckwheat and rye), and increased grain prices incited riots. Post-French Revolution, bread became a symbol of egalitarianism and 'liberte'.

At France's many boulangeries and patisseries people still queue for bread, usually naturally leavened artisan loaves made with ancient wheat, along with buttery brioche, fig bread, pain au chocolat and croissants.

Pierre Hermes's macarons are the stuff of legend, and are worthy of the hype: the fluffy, brightly coloured meringues are filled with rich ganache flavoured with lychee, chocolate, orange blossom and more.

Collecting salt off the coast of Brittany is an ancient practice and fleur de sel ('flower of the sea', its name coming from the patterns of the crystals in the salt crust) is a delicacy used as a garnish, including on eggs, chocolate and fish.

De Gaulle's famous quote sums up French cuisine: this food-loving country does nothing by halves.

CORE INGREDIENTS

HERBS & SPICES
basil, bay leaf, chervil, chive, fennel, herbes de provence, lavender, marjoram, rosemary, saffron, sage, tarragon, thyme

NUTS & SEEDS
almonds, hazelnuts, walnuts

VEGETABLES
asparagus, beetroot (beets), brussels sprouts, capsicum (bell pepper), carrot, eggplant (aubergine), green beans, Jerusalem artichoke, leek, mushroom, pea, potato, shallot, spring onion (scallion), tomato, turnip, zucchini (courgette)

MEATS & SEAFOOD
beef, chicken, duck, fish, frog, horse, lobster, mussel, rabbit, sausage, scallop, snail

FRUITS
apple, apricot, blackberry, blackcurrant, cherry, grape, grapefruit, orange, peach, pear, plum, raspberry, redcurrant, strawberry, tangerine

DAIRY & EGGS
cheese, egg, yoghurt

GRAINS & LEGUMES
haricot beans, lentils, wheat

FATS & OILS
butter, duck fat, olive oil

SPECIALITY & OTHER
bread, fleur de sel, foie gras, mustard, truffle

WINTER

Roasted Apples with Onion Glaze and Gruyère

Ingredients

11 onions

3 litres (101 fl oz/12 cups) premium chicken stock

2 whole parsnips, peeled

4 whole apples, peeled

2 tablespoons grape seed oil

100 g (3½ oz) gruyère

Onions and apples? You bet! Slow-cooking the onions in chicken stock makes them sweet and sticky, like in French onion soup. The apples and parsnips are dynamite together, and the cheese? Well, when has the addition of nutty gruyère ever been a problem?

Method

The day before you plan on serving the dish, peel 10 of the onions and put them in a pot or pan that fits in your oven. Cover with the chicken stock and roast for 8 hours (or overnight) at 90°C (195°F).

The following day, strain and discard the onions and in a stockpot over a high heat reduce the stock, stirring occasionally, for about 1.5 hours or until it has a sweet onion flavour and a more viscous mouth feel. It may need to be seasoned with a touch of salt or sugar to balance it correctly and should coat the back of a spoon.

While the sauce is reducing, preheat the oven to 160°C (320°F). Peel the remaining onion and cut it into 6 wedges, and cut the parsnips into quarters or sixths, depending on their size. Toss the onion, parsnip and apples in the oil, spread out on a baking tray and roast for 45 minutes.

Using a vegetable peeler, peel the cheese into nice long strands. Once the fruit and vegetables are roasted, season them with the onion glaze and place them on a platter. Sprinkle over the gruyere and enjoy.

● VEGETARIAN

Mackerel and Beetroot Niçoise Salad

Ingredients

3 large beetroot (beets)

100 ml (3½ fl oz) good-quality white-wine vinegar

70 g (2½ oz) sugar

400 g (14 oz) mackerel (or other tuna varieties)

50 ml (1¾ fl oz) olive oil

1 cos (romaine) lettuce, washed and chopped into 2 cm (¾ in) pieces

16 pitted black olives

Anchovy dressing

50 g (1¾ oz) anchovies

200 ml (7 fl oz) nut milk

1 bay leaf

70 ml (2¼ fl oz) olive oil

I love to make this dish with albacore, a firm, delicately flavoured white tuna, but, in terms of sustainability, it's not always the best option in Australia. Mackerel is a good swap for tuna as it holds its shape, and the flavours work well with the anchovy dressing. Or try to source sustainable sashimi-grade tuna.

Method

Preheat the oven to 200°C (400°F). Roast 2 of the beetroot whole on a baking tray for 45 minutes, then let cool before peeling and chopping. Set aside.

To make the anchovy dressing, in a small saucepan add the anchovies, nut milk and bay leaf and simmer over a medium–low heat until it has reduced by half. Remove from the heat, take out the bay leaf and add the olive oil. Blitz using a hand-held blender then set aside.

Slice the remaining beetroot as thinly as possible on a mandoline, then put in a metal bowl. In a small saucepan over a high heat, boil the vinegar and sugar with 70 ml (2¼ fl oz) water until the sugar dissolves, then pour over the sliced beetroot and set aside to pickle for at least 20 minutes.

Thinly slice the mackerel, brush it with the olive oil and season with salt. Add the roasted beetroot and lettuce. Spread out some of the pickled beetroot and then garnish the salad with the black olives. Pour over the dressing and serve.

Swordfish Steaks with Pistou and Herb Salad

Ingredients

130 g (4½ oz) hazelnuts

1 garlic clove

100 ml (3½ fl oz) olive oil

1 teaspoon salt

1 bunch basil

1 bunch dill

1 bunch parsley

4 × 160 g (5½ oz) swordfish steaks, at room temperature

Vinaigrette

2 tablespoons hazelnut oil

20 ml (¾ fl oz) white-wine vinegar

30 g (1 oz) wholegrain mustard

Swordfish wild-caught in Australian waters is the more sustainable option than imported swordfish from Asia. It's an underrated fish, full-flavoured and firm, so it holds its shape well. You could substitute with another firm, white fish such as snapper, kingfish or flathead. If you want to quickly turn this into a simple dinner, roasted carrots make a delicious side for this dish.

Method

Preheat the oven to 180°C (350°F). Spread out the hazelnuts on a baking tray and toast in the oven for 10 minutes. Once they're toasted, let them cool a bit and then peel them by placing them in a clean tea towel (dish towel), gathering all the edges of the tea towel in one hand and then rubbing the hazelnuts with your other hand. This will get most of the outer layer to fall off.

Make the pistou by blitzing 80 g (2¾ oz) of the toasted hazelnuts, the garlic, olive oil, salt amd half of each of the bunches of herbs together in a blender. The mixture should be roughly chopped and not too wet.

To make the herb salad, pick the leaves off the remaining herbs and combine in a bowl. Whisk together the vinaigrette ingredients, then fold the vinaigrette through the herbs.

Heat a large pan or griddle over a high heat and cook each swordfish steak on one side until it colours, then flip it and quickly sear the other side. Swordfish eats well quite raw, so you don't need to worry about it being underdone.

Smear a generous amount of the pistou on the plate, then place the fish to one side and the herb salad next to it. Chop the remaining hazelnuts and sprinkle over the top.

Chicken Vin Jaune with Rocket and Carrots

Ingredients

100 g (3½ oz) butter

1 × free-range premium chicken, deboned by your butcher but intact

20 ml (¾ fl oz) grape seed oil

3 garlic cloves, roughly chopped

1 large shallot, diced

3 thyme sprigs

½ rosemary sprig

20 g (¾ oz) dried porcini mushrooms

1 litre (34 fl oz/4 cups) chicken stock

200 ml (7 fl oz) cream

150 ml (5 fl oz) vin jaune or another good-quality white wine

300 g (10½ oz) rocket (arugula), shredded very finely

Roasted white-wine carrots

8 medium carrots halved lengthways

220 ml (7½ fl oz) vin jaune or another good-quality white wine

90 g (3 oz/⅓ cup) butter

2 teaspoons sugar

2 teaspoons salt

So many of us have our own version of roast chicken we love to cook, and this one's mine. It's a warming French classic, made with vin jaune, an oaky, sherry-like wine, from the foothills of the Alps in the Jura region of eastern France. It's the perfect antidote to a cold wintry night. Tip: if you can't get a deboned chicken, just roast a whole chicken following the same steps.

Method

Preheat the oven to 140°C (275°F). Put the butter in the middle of the chicken. Using butcher's twine, tie the chicken up into a ball and put in a roasting tin. It doesn't have to be pretty; you just want it to keep together. Roast the chicken in the oven for 1 hour and 10 minutes, then increase the heat to 230°C (445°F) and roast for 15 more minutes.

While the chicken is roasting, heat the oil in a large saucepan over a medium heat and sauté the garlic and shallot until they are cooked but not coloured. Add the thyme, rosemary, porcini, stock, cream and wine and gently simmer over a medium heat until the sauce has reduced and will coat the back of a spoon. Strain the sauce and return to the saucepan, put the lid on and keep it warm over a very low heat.

Lay the carrots skin side down in a flameproof casserole dish. Add the other ingredients and bring to the boil over a high heat. Put in the oven, uncovered, to reduce for 20 minutes; the carrots will become sticky and acidic.

When the chicken is done, put it on a large platter. Pour over the sauce then scatter the carrots around the chicken and put the rocket to one side to serve.

SPRING

THAILAND

CHINA

INDONESIA

VIETNAM

CAMBODIA

THAILAND

CAPITAL
Bangkok

OFFICIAL LANGUAGE
Thai

AREA
513,120 sq km

POPULATION
68,615,850

CURRENCY
Thai baht

SPRING

Like many countries with multiple culinary influences, Thailand has no 'one dish fits all' to describe its cuisine.

Head to the forested uplands in northern Thailand and expect meaty curries devoid of coconut milk served alongside glutinous sticky rice.

At tiny fishing villages in the fertile centre, where the Chao Phraya River feeds the country's rice paddies, you'll find fragrant noodle soups and steaming bowls of coconut milk curries.

In Bangkok, with its distinctly Chinese influence, expect stir-fries, steamed buns and congee-like rice porridge – along with everything else – at its ever-changing array of street stalls, the quality of which is mind-blowingly good.

Great Thai dishes have bright, vivid flavours and are the perfect balance between sweet, salty, bitter, sour and spicy. Getting that balance right is what makes cooking Thai food such a rewarding experience.

Three of my favourite ingredients to use are Thai basil (a bitey herb with purple stems and an intense licorice-like flavour), kaffir lime leaves (for the aromatic zesty zing they add to any dish), and bird's eye chillies (for their fruity, fiery heat).

CORE INGREDIENTS

HERBS & SPICES
cinnamon, clove, coriander (cilantro), cumin, Chinese five-spice,galangal, kaffir lime, lemongrass, long pepper, pepper, rice paddy herb, spearmint, star anise, Thai basil, turmeric

NUTS & SEEDS
peanuts, prickly ash seeds

VEGETABLES
bean sprouts, chilli, Chinese cabbage, Chinese kale, corn, eggplant (aubergine), garlic, morning glory, shallot, shiitake mushroom, squash, sweet potato, snake (yard-long) beans

MEATS & SEAFOOD
chicken, fish, frog, pork

FRUITS
jackfruit, lime, longan, lychee, mango, mangosteen, papaya, pineapple, pomelo, rambutan

DAIRY & EGGS
condensed milk, egg

GRAINS & NOODLES
jasmine rice, vermicelli noodles

FATS & OILS
coconut oil, peanut oil

SPECIALITY & OTHER
banana flower, coconut milk, fish sauce, palm sugar, shrimp paste, tamarind

SPRING

Oysters with Nam Jim Granita

Ingredients

300 g (10½ oz) cheap table salt

12 shucked oysters

4 kaffir lime leaves, shredded as finely as possible

Nam jim granita

2 long green chillies, seeds removed

1 garlic clove

2 spring onions (scallions), green parts only

juice of 3 limes

20 ml (¾ fl oz) fish sauce

20 g (¾ oz) palm sugar (jaggery)

20 g (¾ oz) coriander (cilantro) leaves

Kaffir lime is as indispensable in Thai cooking as parsley in an Italian nonna's kitchen. When crushed, leaves from this citrus tree are intensely aromatic, adding a unique freshness and vibrancy to food. A tip: If you don't have a kaffir lime tree, you can buy the leaves from an Asian grocer and freeze any you don't use. Nam jim is a traditional Thai dipping sauce reimagined in this recipe as a granita.

Method

Blitz all the granita ingredients together in a blender with 100 ml (3½ fl oz) water, then strain it into a baking tray. Check the seasoning, then put it in the freezer for 2 hours. Once it is an ice block, use a fork to scrape it to become a granita and return it to the freezer until you're ready to serve.

Combine the salt with a bit of water to form a paste. (It's just for presentation, not for eating!) Spread the salt paste out on the serving platter and place the oysters on top. Spoon over the granita and then scatter with the kaffir lime. Serve immediately, as the granita will melt.

Son-in-law Eggs with Chilli Jam and Lime

Ingredients

8 eggs

400 ml (13½ fl oz) oil for frying

100 g (3½ oz) ready-made fried shallots

Chilli jam

3 red shallots, skin on

2 garlic cloves, skin on

2 finger-length red chillies

1 spring onion (scallion)

½ teaspoon ground white pepper

1 bunch Thai basil, leaves picked, plus extra laves to garnish

1 tablespoon palm sugar (jaggery)

1 teaspoon fish sauce

juice of 2 limes

½ bunch coriander, leaves picked

Give your eggs some oomph with this fiery jam. It's loaded with chilli, lime, crunchy shallots and sweet palm sugar, and it's sure to have your palate buzzing. Son-in-law eggs are a Thai staple, where boiled eggs are dunked in hot frying oil to give them a crisp, golden coating.

Method

Bring a saucepan of water to the boil, then carefully add the eggs. Set aside a bowl of ice-water. Boil the eggs for 6 minutes, then refresh them in the ice-water. Peel them under water – the water helps separate the shell from the white, making them easier to peel – and set aside.

To make the chilli jam, set a dry heavy-based frying pan over a high heat. Add the shallots, garlic and chillies, all whole, burn them on each side then remove from the heat. Once the chillies are cool enough to handle, deseed them and then pound them, together with remaining ingredients. Check the seasoning – it never hurts to add a little extra sugar or lime juice, as this mix can be fiery!

In a medium or large frying pan heat the oil to 180°C (350°F) and fry the eggs for about 1 minute, until a golden skin forms on them. Remove from the oil and set on paper towel to drain. Once cool enough to handle, cut a small piece off the top and base of each egg (this means you can stand them up to serve), then cut them in half.

Stand the eggs on the serving platter, then top with the chilli jam. Garnish with the shallots and extra Thai basil and enjoy.

Fish Relish with Tomato and Cucumber

Ingredients

4–12 heirloom tomatoes (depending on size)

1 cucumber

80 g (2¾ oz) ready-made fried shallots

1 bunch Thai basil, leaves picked

Fish relish

50 g (1¾ oz) lemongrass stem, minced

7.5 cm (3 in) piece fresh ginger, minced

3 tomatoes, diced

1 teaspoon ground coriander

1½ teaspoons white pepper

1 kaffir lime leaf, finely shredded

½ teaspoon fennel seeds

juice of 2 limes

1 tablespoon fish sauce

2 teaspoons palm sugar (jaggery)

20 ml (¾ fl oz) grape seed oil

400 g (14 oz) kingfish (or similar white-fleshed fish), filleted

Thai cuisine excels at getting the balance of salty–sour–sweet exactly right and this piquant dish is a top example. It's loaded with punch and texture – crunch from the fried shallots, freshness from the cucumber and tomato, and a flavour explosion from the pounded relish.

Method

In a large non-stick frying pan cook all the relish ingredients except the oil and fish together. It should form a paste.

In a large frying pan over a medium heat, warm the oil then add the fish fillets and sear for about 4 minutes. Repeat for the other side. You actually want to overcook the fish (to help it break down in the relish), so don't be worried. Once the fish is cooked, remove from the heat and set aside.

Cut the tomatoes into some interesting shapes, depending on their size and variety. The cucumber should be sliced on a mandoline into circles about 2 mm (¼ in) thick.

In a large mortar pound the fish and relish together with the pestle and check the seasoning – it should be sweet and sour.

Spoon the relish onto the plate and then place the tomato, cucumber, fried shallots and Thai basil on top to serve.

Eggplant with Tempura Water Spinach and Eggs

Ingredients

2 eggplants (aubergines)

4 eggs

2 tablespoons fish sauce

juice of 3 limes

½ teaspoon honey

400 ml (13½ fl oz) vegetable oil for frying, plus extra for brushing

120 g (4½ oz) rice flour

1 bunch water spinach

Green nam jim

4 green chillies

20 g (¾ oz) coriander (cilantro) root

2 garlic cloves

3 teaspoons sugar

juice of 2 lemons or 3 limes

40 ml (1¼ fl oz) fish sauce

In Thailand, water spinach is eaten raw or tossed in a stir-fry or curry, but I've borrowed the Japanese method of tempura to give this leafy green some crunch. Protein is in the form of boiled eggs, which are super tasty with the smoky eggplant and garlicky chilli dipping sauce nam jim.

Method

Preheat the oven to 200°C (400°F).

To make the nam jim, put all the ingredients in a blender (making sure the coriander root is well washed and free of grit). Blitz until it's a fine purée, then push through a strainer and set aside.

Put the eggplants, whole, on a baking tray and roast for 20 minutes. Remove from the oven, cut them in half and place them back on the tray, skin side down. Brush with a touch of vegetable oil and place back into the oven for another 20 minutes, raising the temperature to 220°C (430°F).

While the eggplants are roasting, bring a small saucepan of water to the boil and add the eggs. Set aside a bowl of ice-water. Boil the eggs for 8 minutes, then cool them in the ice-water for 8 minutes, then remove and peel.

When the eggplants are done roasting, scoop the eggplant flesh out into a bowl and season with the fish sauce, lime juice and honey.

For the tempura, heat the vegetable oil to 180°C (350°F) in a large saucepan. While this is heating up, combine the rice flour and 120 ml (4 fl oz) water in a large bowl. Using your hands, coat the water spinach in the batter then carefully drop into the oil – it won't take long to fry. Remove from the oil and set aside on paper towel.

To serve, place the eggplant down first, then put the egg into the middle. Place a nest of the water spinach around it. Pour the nam jim around the edges and enjoy.

CHINA

CAPITAL
Beijing

OFFICIAL LANGUAGE
Standard Chinese
(Mandarin)

AREA
9,596,960 sq km

POPULATION
1,384,688,960

CURRENCY
yuan

China has given the world some of its best-loved dishes. Steamed xiao long bao (soup dumplings), salt-and-pepper squid, fried rice with sausagey nuggets of lap cheong, and, of course, Peking duck.

Regional styles and specialities define Chinese cuisine, from Cantonese classics (fried rice, chow mein, char siu pork) in southern Guangdong and Hong Kong, to searing Sichuan cuisine loaded with chilli and garlic. Around Shanghai and Jiangsu in eastern China, you'll find lots of fish and red braises (can Chinese spare ribs be any tastier?), but head further north to the coastal province of Shandong and Beijing for fresh, seafood-inspired dishes.

Rice is a major staple, usually steamed, but also fried or glutinous and sticky, wrapped in lotus leaf, eaten at breakfast (as congee) and used to produce beer and vinegar.

Three staple ingredients for Chinese cooking are shaoxing, shiitake and soy sauce. You might have these in your pantry already, but if you don't, stock up.

Shaoxing wine has been made in China for more than 2000 years and adds a sweetness and roundness to a multitude of dishes. Use it to splash in stir-fries or as a marinade for meats. If you're short on shaoxing, dry sherry makes a noble substitute.

Shiitake mushroom, fresh or dried, adds an earthy, umami flavour to Chinese food, and soy sauce (made from fermented soy beans) gives that salty hit.

One thing: cooking Chinese food is fast! Make sure you set the table and have everything organised once you fire up the wok or start cooking. I like to have the ingredients chopped, the sauces measured, and everything ready to roll.

CORE INGREDIENTS

HERBS & SPICES
clove, coriander (cilantro), fennel, Chinese five-spice, garlic, ginger, sesame, sichuan peppercorn, star anise, white pepper

NUTS & SEEDS
peanuts, sesame seeds

VEGETABLES
bamboo shoots, bean sprouts, beans, bok choy, chilli, Chinese broccoli, Chinese eggplant (aubergine), corn, lotus roots, shallot, shiitake, snow peas (mangetout), spring onion (scallion), water chestnuts, watercress, yellow beans

MEATS & SEAFOOD
beef, chicken, duck, fish, oyster, pork, prawn, shrimp, squid

FRUITS
dragon fruit, persimmon, goji berry, lychee, orange

DAIRY & EGGS
egg

GRAINS & NOODLES
black rice, noodles, rice

FATS & OILS
peanut oil, sesame oil

SPECIALITY & OTHER
beer, fermented bean paste, oyster sauce, shaoxing wine, soy sauce, tofu, vinegar, wood ear fungus

SPRING

Bok Choy–Wrapped Oysters with Steamed Garlic and Oyster Sauce

Ingredients

18 shucked oysters

140 ml (4½ fl oz) oyster sauce

8 large garlic cloves, 4 minced and 4 thinly sliced

1 tablespoon grape seed oil

12 bok choy (pak choy)

Oyster, bok choy, garlic – what a combo! These one-bite parcels are a fancy Chinese canapé that might seem complicated to make but are actually pretty easy. Presenting hot, saucy oysters in their steamed green parcels is a guaranteed party pleaser.

Method

In a blender blitz 6 of the oysters, the oyster sauce, minced garlic, oil and 60 ml (2 fl oz/¼ cup) water. Pour the sauce into a non-stick pan over a medium–high heat and simmer for 5 minutes. Set aside.

Bring a large saucepan of water to the boil. There should be enough water to cover the stems of the bok choy but not the leaves if they are upright in the pan. Set aside a large bowl of ice-water. Place the bok choy upright in the pan, put the lid on and turn off the heat. Wait 40 seconds, then put the bok choy into the ice-water to refresh and cool. Cut the leaves off the bok choy and set the leaves aside. Open the boy choy (if you're having trouble with this, you can use a small sharp knife, to hollow out the centre of the bok choy stems) and place an oyster and a couple of slices of garlic in each one, then tightly roll the stuffed bok choy in its leaves.

Place a bamboo steamer on top of the pan you were using before and bring the water to a simmer. Put the bok choy parcels in the steamer and steam for 2 minutes.

To serve, stand all the bok choy up on a plate and then pour over the sauce. This dish is best steamed to order.

Crunchy Fried Rice with Scallop and Egg

Ingredients

6 eggs

600 g (1 lb 5 oz) steamed rice

65 ml (2¼ oz) vegetable oil

1 bunch spring onions (scallions), 4 minced, the rest thinly sliced, green parts only

2 cm (¾ in) piece fresh ginger, finely diced

4 garlic cloves

4 large scallops, diced

2 lap cheong, diced

¼ teaspoon light soy sauce

¼ teaspoon sesame oil

2 teaspoons shaoxing rice wine

⅓ bunch coriander (cilantro), finely shredded

I've never eaten Chinese without ordering fried rice – I absolutely love it. This is a simple, forgiving recipe you can adapt to whatever's in your pantry. Make it with only two or three vegetables, or turn it into a luxe feast with seafood and sausage. Lap cheong is dried Chinese pork sausage, flavoured with soy and wine, and has a sweet and savoury taste. It's available from Asian grocers, but you can substitute it with a good-quality ham if need be.

Method

Whisk the eggs together. In a large bowl, gently combine half the egg with the rice to coat. In a wok over a high heat, pour in half the oil and get it very hot. Add the remaining egg mix and let it set for about 5 seconds, then quickly scramble and set aside in a bowl.

In the same wok over a medium heat, pour in the other half of the oil and add the minced spring onion, the ginger and garlic and sauté, but don't burn. Add in the rice and turn the heat up high. Mix very quickly so it fries nicely, adding the scallops and the lap cheong.

Once the rice starts to separate into individual grains, add in the light soy, sesame oil and shaoxing rice wine and remove from the heat.

Turn the rice out on a platter, then sprinkle over the coriander and the remaining spring onion.

Fragrant Eggplant

Ingredients

6 large eggplants (aubergines)

30 g (1 oz) salt

100 g (3½ oz) sugar

100 g (3½ oz) honey

50 ml (1¾ oz) Chinese black vinegar

50 ml (1¾ fl oz) light soy sauce

7.5 cm (3 in) piece fresh ginger, minced

1 garlic clove, minced

1 teaspoon chilli flakes

50 g (1¾ oz) fermented bean paste

2 finger-length red chillies, minced

vegetable oil for deep-frying

400 g (14 oz) rice flour

2 spring onions (scallions), thinly sliced, to garnish

Oh yeah, baby! Eggplant lovers, put this on your hit list. The fried crispness of the skin, the softness of the flesh, the sweetness of the honey, and the earthy depth of the fermented bean paste (a salty, savoury condiment made from ground soybeans) meld together to create something awesome. Black vinegar, also known as Chinkiang vinegar, is found on the tables at most Chinese dumpling restaurants and is readily available.

Method

Cut each eggplant into 6–8 wedges. Put them in a large bowl, cover with the salt and leave them for 20 minutes. This pulls out the moisture and makes them fry better.

In a saucepan combine the sugar and honey and bring to a boil over a medium–high heat. Once the mixture coats the back of a spoon and the sugar is dissolved, remove from the heat and add the vinegar, soy sauce, ginger, garlic, chilli flakes, bean paste and half the chilli, and whisk. Set aside.

In a large saucepan over a high heat, preheat the oil to 180°C (350°F). Spread the rice flour out in a shallow bowl. Gently squeeze the salt water from the eggplant and then roll in the rice flour to coat. Fry the eggplant until crisp, then plate with the sauce and garnish with the spring onion and remaining chilli.

● VEGETARIAN

Green Beans with Peanut and Shiitake Mushroom Crumble

Ingredients

150 ml (5 fl oz) grape seed oil

16 shiitake mushrooms, roughly sliced

2 garlic cloves, minced

2 cm (¾ in) piece fresh ginger, minced

60 ml (2 fl oz/¼ cup) soy sauce

20 ml (¾ fl oz) Chinese black vinegar

100 g (3½ oz) crushed peanuts

500 g (1 lb 2 oz) green beans

A top-notch dish with gutsy flavours, which are sometimes found lacking in vegetarian cooking. The 'meatiness' comes from the earthy umami-ness of the shiitake mushrooms and the malty smokiness of the black vinegar (also called Chinkiang vinegar). Make sure you really blister the beans to get the right crunch and texture.

Method

In a wok or frying pan over a medium–high heat, warm 50 ml (1¾ fl oz) of the oil. Sauté the mushrooms until lightly coloured, then remove from the heat and chop them into a rough mince. Set aside.

In the same pan, over a high heat, warm another 50 ml (1¾ fl oz) of oil and fry the garlic and ginger until golden and crispy. Add in the soy sauce and vinegar and the shiitake mushrooms, and cook, stirring, until the mushrooms are cooked. Mix in the crushed peanuts and set aside.

Again place the same pan over the highest possible heat and pour in the remaining oil. When the oil is hot, stir-fry the beans until the skin blisters but the beans aren't overcooked.

Pile the beans and peanut and shiitake crumble onto a plate to serve.

● VEGAN

INDONESIA

CAPITAL
Jakarta

OFFICIAL LANGUAGE
Bahasa Indonesia

AREA
1,904,570 sq km

POPULATION
262,787,400

CURRENCY
Indonesian rupiah

More than 300 ethnic groups live on the hundreds of islands comprising the tropical Indonesian archipelago, Java and Sumatra being the most densely populated.

Indonesia's geographic position in the 'ring of fire', an area of the Pacific Ocean where volcanoes erupt and earthquakes are probable, means its soil is incredibly fertile. Hiking Bali's highest peak, the active stratovolcano of Mount Agung, to see the sunrise is amazing – but even more so is seeing the growers and their thriving crops of chillies and flowers.

The hot and humid coastal lowlands are covered with rice paddies, vegetable crops (such as corn and cassava), and tropical fruits, including mangosteen, jackfruit and rambutan. Coffee grows in the cooler forested hinterlands of the larger islands.

Indonesians love their food. You'll find markets teeming with fresh fruit, and a convivial vibe at the *warungs* (open-air, informal restaurants).

Street vendors are everywhere, selling skewers of chicken satay, tamarind fish soup, gado gado and coconut pancakes, or *padang* food from West Sumatra, such as the famed rendang curry.

Rice is the centrepiece of a typical Indonesian meal, often eaten with dried fish and homemade sambal. This spicy-hot sauce made with chillies and fermented shrimp paste is a staple condiment that accompanies most food, from fish to raw veg.

Islam is the majority religion, but Hindu and Chinese-Indonesian influence brings the pork, including Indonesia's famed *babi guling*, which translates as 'turning pig'. The cavity of a suckling pig is rubbed with a gutsy, garlicky spice mix of turmeric, lemongrass, chilli, ginger, tamarind (and more), and roasted over an open fire on a hand-turned spit. If roasting an entire pig feels too advanced, fair enough! My recipe for Pork jowl with tamarind sambal and garlic spinach (page 197) is inspired by *babi guling*, but is hopefully more achievable.

CORE INGREDIENTS

HERBS & SPICES
black pepper, cassava leaves, clove, galangal, garlic, lemongrass, mace, nutmeg, pandan leaves, tamarind, turmeric

NUTS & SEEDS
candlenuts, peanuts

VEGETABLES
cabbage, calabash, carrot, cassava, cauliflower, chayote, chilli, corn, eggplant (aubergine), potato, shallot, snake (yard-long) beans, spinach, sweet potato, taro, yam

MEATS & SEAFOOD
anchovy, beef, chicken, goat, mackerel, mussels, pork, snapper, squid, tuna

FRUITS
breadfruit, durian, jackfruit, mango, mangosteen, pawpaw, rambutan, soursop, starfruit

DAIRY & EGGS
egg

GRAINS & NOODLES
noodles, rice, wheat

SPECIALITY & OTHER
coconut, fermented shrimp paste, palm sugar, sambal, tofu

SPRING

Prawns with Sambal and Pineapple

Ingredients

8 prawns, halved lengthways

20 ml (¾ fl oz) grape seed oil

1 pineapple, diced, core removed

1 bunch coriander (cilantro), leaves picked

juice of 2 limes

Sambal

10 red chillies, deseeded and minced

4 large shallots, minced

4 garlic cloves, minced

20 ml (¾ fl oz) fish sauce

20 g (¾ oz) sugar

5 g (¼ oz) lemongrass stem, minced

60 ml (2 fl oz/¼ cup) peanut oil

3 kaffir lime leaves

Perfecting the art of the barbecued prawn is an Aussie rite of passage, and I love this method of slicing them lengthways so they're easy to eat, yet beautifully presented. Here, the high-impact sambal is the star of the show, so take the time to get the sweet–salty balance spot on.

Method

In a mortar and pestle pound all the sambal ingredients except the peanut oil and the kaffir lime leaves. Continue pounding as you pour in the peanut oil. Once it looks like a paste, cook it gently in a non-stick pan with the lime leaves, stirring until the paste darkens and thickens. Taste and perhaps add some extra fish sauce or sugar, depending on whether you need extra saltiness or sweetness, then set aside.

Brush the prawns with the oil. Put a griddle or barbecue on a high heat, then cook the prawns, shell side down, until they are just starting to cook through, then remove from the heat. Next grill the pineapple quickly, just for a touch of heat and flavour.

In a large bowl, mix the pineapple though the coriander, lime juice and sambal. Arrange the prawns on a platter, then cover with the pineapple, herb and sambal mix. Enjoy!

Chicken Skewers with Satay Sauce and Tomato Salad

Ingredients

6 chicken thighs, skin on, diced then skewered

100 g (3½ oz) roasted peanuts, crushed to a powder

Satay sauce

50 ml (1¾ fl oz) grape seed oil

5 garlic cloves, crushed

1 white onion, chopped

1 red chilli, seeds removed

1 teaspoon sugar

130 g (4½ oz) peanut butter

Tomato salad

10 g (¼ oz) palm sugar (jaggery)

juice of 2 limes

25 ml (¾ fl oz) peanut oil

300 g (10½ oz) heirloom tomatoes, diced

100 g (3½ oz) spinach

'Stick food' is an all-time favourite at many a gathering, and plump grilled chicken basted in spicy satay is a sure-fire winner. Creamy, coconutty and rich, this peanut-based sauce is balanced by the freshness of tomato and spinach with a zingy lime dressing.

Method

To make the satay sauce, in a food processor blitz the ingredients along with 350 ml (12 fl oz) water. Pour the mixture into a large frying pan and slowly cook over a low heat until it's fragrant and the onion flavour tastes cooked. The sauce shouldn't be too thick.

Prepare the salad dressing by heating 30 ml (1 fl oz) water in a small saucepan and adding in the palm sugar until it dissolves. Whisk in the lime juice and peanut oil and set aside.

Heat up your barbecue, or if you're using an oven, preheat it to 200°C (400°F). Brush the skewers heavily with the satay sauce. Barbecue the skewers over a high heat for 8 minutes, or roast them on a baking tray in the oven for about 12 minutes.

Pile the salad on the plate, pour over the dressing, sprinkle over the crushed peanuts and place the hot skewers on top. Serve any extra satay sauce on the side.

Pork Jowl with Tamarind Sambal and Garlic Spinach

Ingredients

2 whole pork jowls (cheeks)

8 garlic cloves, 3 whole and 5 sliced

7.5 cm (3 in) piece fresh ginger

5 black peppercorns

2 star anise

2 cinnamon sticks

100 ml (3½ fl oz) grape seed oil

500 g (1 lb 2 oz) spinach

1 teaspoon ground white pepper

Tamarind sambal

40 g (1½ oz) seedless tamarind pulp

2 finger-length red chillies

2 shallots, roughly chopped

1 garlic clove

½ tomato

2 tablespoons peanut oil

pinch of salt

juice of ½ lime

Inspired by *babi guling* **(whole suckling pig spit-roasted over an open fire), this recipe calls for pork jowl, a fatty, cheap cut that is utterly delicious when slow-cooked. The bittersweet tamarind sambal ties the dish together. You can make the sambal as spicy as you like by whizzing up more chillies, but you may need to add more peanut oil to keep the consistency from being too thick.**

Method

Preheat the oven to 200°C (400°F). Put the pork jowls in a deep roasting tin and roast for 30 minutes.

While this is cooking, add 2.5 litres (85 fl oz/10 cups) water with the whole garlic cloves, ginger, peppercorns, star anise and cinnamon to a stockpot and boil for 20 minutes to create a quick stock. Once the pork is cooked, pour the stock over and cover the tray with foil. Reduce the heat to 150°C (300°F) and roast for another 1.5 hours.

Heat the oil to around 60°C (140°F) a small saucepan over a low heat. Add the sliced garlic and cook for 15 minutes; don't colour the garlic in any way. Remove from the heat and set aside, letting the garlic infuse the oil.

For the sambal, pulse everything together in a blender.

Let the pork cool to room temperature (approximately 30 minutes) and slice it into 120 g (4½ oz) steaks. (You may need to remove some fat.) Place the pork cut side down in a large non-stick pan and bring to a medium heat. It should cook like bacon and caramelise beautifully.

Remove the pork and, in the same pan, add the spinach and sauté over a high heat. Pour over a touch of the garlic oil and season with the pepper.

To serve, spread some sambal on the plate, place the pork on it and cover it with the sautéed garlic spinach and remaining garlic oil.

Squid with Fresh Fruit Sambal and Squid Ink Sauce

Ingredients

120 ml (4 fl oz) peanut oil

2 large shallots, minced

5 garlic cloves, minced

12 finger-length red chillies, seeds removed and minced

7.5 cm (3 in) piece fresh ginger, diced

80 ml (2½ fl oz/⅓ cup) good-quality fish sauce

1 mango, finely diced

4 lychees, peeled and finely diced

2 mangosteens or a small amount of pineapple, finely diced

1 tomato, roughly chopped

3 limes, 1 segmented and then minced, 2 juiced

120 g (4½ oz/¾ cup) peanuts, roughly chopped

60 ml (2 fl oz) squid ink (optional)

1 large squid, at room temperature

80 g (2¾ oz) ready-made fried shallots

Cleaning whole squid (by removing its quill, beak, membrane and entrails) can be a step too far for many home cooks. There are loads of YouTube videos if you fancy giving it a crack, but if you're not comfortable, ask your fishmonger to clean the squid for you. You can leave the squid ink out of this recipe if you prefer; the colour won't be black, but it's still delicious.

Method

Put 2 tablespoons of the peanut oil in a frying pan over a medium–high heat, then add the shallot, garlic and chillies and cook, stirring occasionally, until they begin to darken. Add the diced ginger and 2 tablespoons of the fish sauce and remove from the heat.

Put the mango, lychees, mangosteens, tomato and minced lime in a large bowl, and combine with half of the shallot mixture to make the fresh fruit sambal, and set aside.

When it's cooled down enough to blend, in a blender blitz the other half of the sambal mixture with the peanuts, lime juice, squid ink and 40 ml (1¼ fl oz) of the peanut oil until you have a thin black sauce.

Get a wok or large frying pan nice and hot and sear the squid with the remaining peanut oil for 1 minute on each side. Pour the remaining fish sauce over the squid and remove from the heat.

Splash the black sauce across the plate, followed by the fresh fruit sambal. Top with the squid, garnish with the shallots, and dig in.

VIETNAM

CAPITAL
Hanoi

OFFICIAL LANGUAGE
Vietnamese

AREA
331,210 sq km

POPULATION
97,040,330

CURRENCY
Vietnamese dong

Pho, rice-paper rolls, *banh mi*! Do these faves define Vietnamese food? Yes and no. Food in Vietnam is fresh, vivid and fragrant – a balance of sour, sweet, salty, bitter and spicy – but it's a cuisine hard to pin down, influenced by its neighbours, geography and French colonisation until 1954.

In the cool, hilly regions up north, Chinese and Laotian techniques are found in dishes such as rice noodles with marinated pork, or crab noodle soup. Vietnamese cuisine shares ingredients, such as lemongrass, fish sauce, rice and palm sugar, with its southern neighbours, Cambodia and Thailand. And behold the *banh mi*, a crusty, fluffy baguette stuffed with pickled daikon, chilli and pork or tofu that's French-Vietnamese fusion in a bun.

SPRING

The murky waters of the Mekong Delta, Vietnam's rice bowl and the major source of the country's fish, is home to the colourful floating markets, where locals peddle their fruit, veg and flowers on boats–turned–market stalls.

Pho (surely Vietnam's national dish?) is found throughout the country, with regional tweaks along the way. Fewer fresh herbs are added in the north, and the length of time simmering the stock can vary from six to 48 hours. The technique of making the stock – roasting beef or chicken bones simmered in water with spices such as star anise and ginger – has its roots in French and Chinese cookery. The result is an utterly fragrant, soul-nourishing soup that inspired my 'pho seasoning' for the Wagyu beef pho tartare (page 207).

CORE INGREDIENTS

HERBS & SPICES
betel leaf, cassia, chilli, chive, clove, galangal, lemongrass, star anise, tamarind, turmeric, Vietnamese mint

NUTS & SEEDS
peanuts, sesame seeds

VEGETABLES
asparagus, bean sprouts, cabbage, carrot, cucumber, daikon, potato, shallot, spring onion (scallion), tomato, water spinach, watercress

MEATS & SEAFOOD
beef, chicken, crab, duck, pork, prawn, squid

FRUITS
lime, pineapple, pomelo

DAIRY & EGGS
egg

GRAINS & NOODLES
rice, vermicelli noodles

FATS & OILS
pork fat, sesame oil

SPECIALITY & OTHER
baguette, bamboo shoots, coconut juice, fish sauce, palm sugar, rice paper, shrimp paste, tofu

SPRING

Boiled Egg with Asparagus, Lettuce and Fish Sauce Butter

Ingredients

4 eggs

40 ml (1¼ fl oz) dark soy sauce

40 ml (1¼ fl oz) Vietnamese premium fish sauce

120 g (4½ oz) butter, diced

juice of 2 limes

12 large and thick asparagus spears, or 20 thin

2 tablespoons vegetable oil

½ iceberg lettuce, quartered

This French-leaning dish may seem a bit weird with the addition of fish sauce, but the cold crunch of lettuce counterbalanced by hot, salty egg and the buttery, full-bodied sauce paired with asparagus works perfectly.

Method

Bring a saucepan of water to the boil and set aside a bowl of ice-water. Add the eggs to the pan and boil for 8 minutes, then refresh in the ice-water bath. Peel them under water – the water helps separate the shell from the white, making them easier to peel. Then slice the eggs thinly and evenly, keeping the yolk and white together, place in a shallow dish and cover with the dark soy sauce.

In a saucepan over a medium–low heat bring the fish sauce and 80 ml (2½ fl oz/⅓ cup) water to the boil, then remove from the heat and whisk through the butter and the lime juice. Set aside, but keep it warm.

Arrange the asparagus in a large frying pan and drizzle over the oil. Put over a high heat and semi-burn them on one side. Remove from the heat and season with salt. Chop the asparagus into small pieces then mix through the egg.

To serve, lay the iceberg down on the plate. Spoon the egg and asparagus mixture all over the lettuce, then pour over the fish sauce butter.

Octopus and Pomelo Salad with Sweet Potato

Ingredients

2 sweet potatoes

2 baby octopus

1 garlic bulb, halved

7.5 cm (3 in) piece fresh ginger

1 lemongrass stem

¼ pineapple, sliced

2 spring onions (scallions), finely sliced

100 g (3½ oz) toasted peanuts, lightly crushed

1 pomelo or grapefruit, broken into small segments

1 tablespoon vegetable oil

40 ml (1¼ fl oz) fish sauce

1 teaspoon chilli flakes

2 teaspoons rice vinegar

1 bunch Vietnamese mint

80 g (2¾ oz) ready-made fried shallots

Dressing

50 g (1¾ oz) palm sugar (jaggery)

1 lemongrass stem, white part only, minced

1 bird's eye chilli, thinly sliced

1 garlic clove, minced

juice of 3 limes

85 ml (2¾ fl oz) premium fish sauce

Stay with me here. Yes, this is a long-ish recipe, and yes, there are a few processes involved, but each step is easy to achieve and, with a little organisation, you'll be able to pull off this dish no worries. Trust me, it's worth it. The pale pink tartness of the pomelo with the succulent, lightly pickled char-grilled octopus, and the tangy pineapple with peanuts and chilli makes for a showstopper.

Method

Preheat the oven to 180°C (350°F). Wrap the sweet potatoes in foil and roast in the oven for 45 minutes, then set aside in their foil.

Bring a large saucepan of water to the boil and set aside a large bowl of ice-water. Dip the octopus in the boiling water for 3 minutes and then submerge it in the ice-water. Repeat three times. (This process washes the octopus as much as it tenderises it.)

Half-fill a stockpot with water and add the octopus, the garlic bulb, ginger and lemongrass. Bring this to a simmer and cook for 1.5 to 2 hours. Pull out a tentacle as you go and cut a small piece off to test the tenderness. It should be soft and delicate, not chewy. Once it's ready, pour out most of the water but make sure the octopus is still covered. Drop in a few ice cubes and let it cool to room temperature.

To make the dressing, melt the palm sugar in 70 ml (¼ fl oz) warm water in a small bowl, then mix in the remaining dressing ingredients and set aside.

In a large bowl combine the pineapple, spring onion, peanuts and pomelo and set aside.

Unwrap the sweet potato and roughly break it into pieces. Break the octopus down into four pieces (with two tentacles each). In a large non-stick pan over a high heat, add the vegetable oil and sear the octopus to get a stunning colour on it. Pour over the fish sauce, chilli flakes and vinegar and remove from the heat. Add in the sweet potato.

Remove the sweet potato from the octopus mixture and place it on the plate first. Combine the pomelo mixture and the dressing, then add to the plate. Arrange the octopus on top so you can really show it off. Garnish with the Vietnamese mint and fried shallots and serve.

Wagyu Beef Pho Tartare

Ingredients

200 ml (7 fl oz) grape seed oil,
plus extra for searing beef

2 sheets dried rice paper

80 g (2¾ oz) rice

2 cm (¾ in) lemongrass stem

400 g (14 oz) premium wagyu beef,
in 1 cm (½ in) thick slices

4 baby onions, halved

4 egg yolks

Pho seasoning

100 ml (3½ fl oz) oil

2 garlic cloves, minced

1 cm (½ in) piece fresh ginger, minced

2 shallots, minced

½ teaspoon chilli powder

½ teaspoon ground cloves

½ teaspoon ground cinnamon

½ teaspoon ground coriander

2 teaspoons fish sauce

There are a few processes to this recipe, which is more dinner-party special than fast midweek feed. It's my take on traditional Vietnamese pho, the brothy noodle soup found throughout the country. Toasting the rice is a common Asian cookery hack, used to add texture and a smoky, nutty flavour to dishes. If you've ever made pappadums, you'll be a pro at frying the rice paper, which uses a similar technique. Watching the rice paper puff up is fun – and fast! – but take care, as the oil is super hot.

Method

To make the pho seasoning, in a small saucepan over a low heat warm the oil and add the garlic, ginger and shallot. Combine the spices and fish sauce in a large heatproof bowl and place it next to the stove. Raise the heat to high and whisk the garlic and ginger oil – you want it to cook until it is golden and even, not burnt in any way! Once it's golden, carefully pour the oil straight over the spices and fish sauce and set aside to cool.

In a large saucepan over a high heat, bring the grape seed oil up to just pre smoking point. You can check if it's the right heat by dipping a small offcut of the rice paper into the oil with tongs. If it puffs up like a prawn cracker, it's the right temperature. Using tongs, one by one dip the rice paper in the oil. Once it puffs up, carefully pull it out and reserve on paper towel. Be really careful doing this – it shouldn't take more than a couple of seconds, but it's really hot! Set aside the pan of oil to cool somewhere out of the way.

To toast the rice, place it in a dry frying pan with just the lemongrass for aroma. On a high heat, keep moving the rice until it is evenly golden. (You can also toast the rice by roasting it in the oven at 160°C/320°F for 40 minutes.) Allow to cool slightly, then remove from the pan and in a blender blitz to a fine powder.

Put a large frying pan on a high heat. Once it's almost smoking, pour a tiny amount of oil in and sear one side of the beef only. This is just for additional flavour, so don't actually cook it. The faster you do this step the better. Set aside the beef. Keeping the pan over a high heat, next put the onions in, cut side down, burning them. Turn the heat off and let them keep cooking while you dice the seared beef using a sharp knife.

Once the oil from frying the rice paper has cooled to 70°C (160°F), dip a spoon in it, then place an egg yolk on the spoon and dip it in the oil. You can likely fit four spoons – so all four yolks – in the pan at once. The confit should take less than 4 minutes. To check whether the yolk is done, pull it out of the oil and feel it; you want it runny but not raw. Set aside on paper towel or baking paper.

Place the confit egg yolk in the middle of the plate. Season the diced beef to your liking with the pho seasoning mix and arrange it around the yolk. Pop out the shells of the onion and place on top, place shards of the puffed rice paper around the plate and then dust with the rice powder.

Whiting with Nuoc Cham Sauce, Pickled Vegetables and Herbs

Ingredients

4 whole small whiting or 2 large filleted whiting

1 bunch mixed Asian herbs, picked

Pickled vegetables

4 carrots, peeled

1 large daikon, peeled

150 ml (5 fl oz) vinegar

100 g (3½ oz) sugar

Nuoc cham

2 tablespoons sugar

2 bird's eye chillies, thinly sliced (seeds removed if you want less heat)

1 garlic clove, minced

juice of 2 limes

85 ml (2¾ fl oz) premium fish sauce

Adding simple extras, such as nuoc cham and pickled veg, transforms plain old 'fish and salad' into a restaurant-quality dish. Nuoc cham, a salty–spicy–sweet dipping sauce, is a classic accompaniment throughout Vietnam. For the mixed herbs, use coriander (cilantro), Vietnamese mint, fish herb, rice paddy herb – whatever you can find!

Method

To make the pickles, cut the vegetables into the longest, nicest rectangular strips you can and put them in a heatproof bowl. Put 150 ml (5 fl oz) of water into a saucepan with the vinegar and sugar, bring it to the boil until the sugar dissolves, then pour over the carrot and daikon and set aside.

Make the nuoc cham by dissolving the sugar in 100 ml (3½ fl oz) warm water in a small bowl and set aside. In another small bowl combine all the other nuoc cham ingredients. Once the sugar water is back to room temperature, pour it into the bowl with the rest of the nuoc cham ingredients – it's important the water is room temperature so you don't cook the lime juice in any way.

Get a large frying pan or skillet very hot, then sear the whiting fillets, skin side down. If you have one, put a heatproof weight on the fish so the skin crisps evenly. We are looking for them to be golden brown, approximately 3 minutes. Season the flesh side, and once the fish is almost cooked through flip it and then take it straight out of the pan.

To serve, place the pickles randomly on the plate, then add the fish. Mix the herbs thoroughly through the nuoc cham and cover the dish with it. Serve the remainder of the nuoc cham on the side as a dipping sauce.

CAMBODIA

CAPITAL
Phnom Penh

OFFICIAL LANGUAGE
Khmer

AREA
181,030 sq km

POPULATION
16,449,520

CURRENCY
Cambodian riel

Khmer cuisine has all the hallmarks of its fellow South-East Asian compadres: bright, colourful, aromatic dishes loaded with fresh herbs, with a balance of salty, sweet, spicy, sour and bitter flavours.

The mighty Mekong River and large freshwater lake Tonle Sap are Cambodia's greatest resources, sustaining hundreds of rice paddies and providing the country with a rich supply of freshwater fish. Fish is fermented and dried, sold at pungent-smelling shops, and turned into fragrant soups, textural salads and coconut curries.

Chinese and French influence are dominant in Cambodian cuisine and crusty, fresh baguettes are easily found, along with pork belly and Chinese techniques such as steaming and stir-frying.

SPRING

Kampot pepper – or 'black gold' – is grown organically in the quartz-rich foothills of the Elephant Mountains, and has been cultivated in the Kampot region since about the thirteenth century. This highly prized pepper, with its mild caramelly flavour, is considered some of the world's best. I use it in my recipe for Steamed white fish with kampot pepper and kaffir lime (page 219), and it's available online and from good spice shops.

Another ingredient typical of Cambodian cooking is bitter melon, also known as 'wild cucumber', a tropical vine of South-East Asia. Its vitamin-packed, bitter-tasting, gourd-like fruit looks like a lumpy cucumber and is thought to help lower blood sugar. It's commonly used in stir-fries, but can also be boiled or braised. Find it at Asian grocers.

CORE INGREDIENTS

HERBS & SPICES
black pepper, chilli, garlic, ginger, kampot pepper, star anise, turmeric

NUTS & SEEDS
cashew nuts, lotus seeds

VEGETABLES
bitter melon, bok choy, cabbage, corn, luffa, mushroom, snake (yard-long) beans, snow pea (mangetout), spring onion (scallion), squash, tomato, water spinach, winter melon

MEATS & SEAFOOD
fish, pork, prawn

FRUITS
apple, cumquat, custard apple, guava, jackfruit, lemon, longan, lychee, mango, mangosteen, papaya, persimmon, pineapple, plum, pomelo, soursop, starfruit, watermelon

DAIRY & EGGS
egg

GRAINS & NOODLES
egg noodles, rice, rice noodles

FATS & OILS
pork fat

SPECIALITY & OTHER
bamboo shoots, coconut, palm sugar, sugarcane

SPRING

Watermelon Salad with Peppered Pickles

Ingredients

100 ml (3½ fl oz) oil for frying

15 g (½ oz/½ cup) curry leaves

1 watermelon, balled with
a melon baller

12 cherry tomatoes, halved

Peppered pickles

4 radishes, cut into sixths

½ bitter melon, balled with
a melon baller

1 squash, cut into 16 wedges

1 persimmon, peeled and diced

1 shallot, sliced

1 star anise

1 teaspoon black peppercorns

190 g (6½ oz) palm sugar (jaggery)

1 teaspoon ground turmeric

300 ml (10 fl oz) rice vinegar

20 g (¾ oz) salt

There's a perception that pickling is an involved process that takes months to achieve, but in Asian cooking veggies are often pickled and eaten soon after. I've suggested you wait an hour or so to let the pickles cool, but then go for it. You'll love the freshness and lightness of just-pickled veg, which gives a gentle crunch to this salad, and perfectly balances the sweet watermelon.

Method

For the pickles, first sanitise a large glass jar by washing it with soapy water, then pouring fresh boiling water in it. Pour the water out, then put the radish, bitter melon, squash, persimmon and shallot in the jar. Put 300 ml (10 fl oz) water into a saucepan and add the star anise, peppercorns, palm sugar, turmeric, rice vinegar and salt. Bring it to the boil and pour over the pickles.
Put the lid on and let the pickles sit for at least an hour.

While the pickles do their thing, pour the oil in a frying pan over a high heat and fry the curry leaves. Once the oil is the right temperature it won't take more than 30 seconds to fry the leaves. Set aside.

Once the pickles have cooled down and softened, strain them and mix them in a bowl with the watermelon and tomato. Dress with a touch of the pickle liquid. Once combined, plate the salad, garnish with the curry leaves and serve!

● VEGAN

Stuffed Mushrooms with Chive and Black Pepper Butter

Ingredients

150 g (5½ oz) butter

20 ml (¾ fl oz) soy sauce

½ bunch chives, finely sliced into circles

1 star anise, ground

½ teaspoon ground black pepper

610 g (1 lb 6 oz) shiitake mushrooms

120 g (4½ oz) cashew nuts, crushed

Settle back and wait for the compliments to roll in with this super simple mushroom dish that packs a mighty umami punch. I ate something similar to this recipe in Cambodia and it blew my mind with its easy technique and flavourful heft. I hope you enjoy it as much as I do.

Method

Preheat the oven to 185°C (365°F). First soften the butter to room temperature, then in a bowl combine the butter with the soy sauce, chives, star anise and pepper to create a paste. Stuff the mushrooms with the paste, put them on a baking tray and roast them for 10 minutes.

Scatter over the cashew nuts to serve.

● VEGETARIAN

Pipis with Ginger and Spring Onion Sauce

Ingredients

40 ml (1¼ fl oz) peanut oil

2 teaspoons sesame oil

2 banana shallots, diced

5 garlic cloves, minced

70 g (2½ oz) fresh ginger, julienned
on a mandoline

350 ml (12 fl oz) chicken stock

2 teaspoons sugar

2 long red chillies, deseeded
and sliced into thin strips

1 kg (2 lb 3 oz) pipis or clams
(vongole)

1 bunch spring onions (scallions),
sliced into thin rings

20 ml (¾ fl oz) light soy sauce

Healthy, fast and simple, this dish is a warming favourite and uses a typical combination of Asian flavours. Serve it over steamed rice for an easy dinner option. You can buy chicken stock, but I prefer to use homemade stock, as it's a better, rounder flavour. It's easy to make: next time you have a roast chook, cover the carcass with water and simmer with celery tops, carrot and peeled onion for about 25 minutes, strain, let cool and freeze until you need it.

Method

In a large non-stick frying pan with a lid, warm the peanut and sesame oils over a medium heat. Add in the shallot, garlic and ginger and sauté. You don't want the ingredients to colour. Add the chicken stock, sugar and chillies and bring to the boil, then add the pipis and put the lid on the pan.

Once the pipis have opened, add in the spring onion and the soy sauce and serve.

Steamed White Fish with Kampot Pepper and Kaffir Lime

Ingredients

2 banana leaves, halved

1 lemongrass stem, white part only

4 large slices fresh ginger

6 spring onions (scallions)

4 fillets best-quality white fish (ideally flathead)

4 kaffir lime leaves

30 g (1 oz) kampot pepper (or black pepper)

30 g (1 oz) salt

2 lime cheeks

Unwrapping a banana leaf parcel of fragrant fish creates an interactive sense of drama to an otherwise simple dish. Asking your guests to add their own garnish is a nice touch, too. You can source banana leaves at Asian grocers or online. Same deal with kampot pepper, which has a mild, almost caramel flavour and doesn't overpower the fish.

Method

First spread out the banana leaf halves on a clean flat surface. Cut the lemongrass stem into quarters and then divide across the banana leaves, followed by the slices of ginger. Quarter the whites of 4 spring onions the same way as the lemongrass and place in the centre of the leaves. Put the fish on top and wrap the banana leaf around the fish. Tie the parcels with some kitchen string. To steam the fish, place a tight-fitting bamboo steamer on top of a large saucepan of boiling water. Steam the fish for 6–8 minutes with the lid on.

Shred the green parts of the remaining spring onion and kaffir lime leaves as finely as possible, and put them in a small serving bowl.

Using a spice grinder or a very dry blender, finely grind the pepper and salt together.

Place the kampot pepper mix, lime cheeks and bowl of spring onion greens and kaffir lime leaves in the middle of the table. Place the banana leaf parcels on the plate and let your guests unwrap it themselves. Your guests can garnish to taste.

Thank you

I would firstly like to thank my family: my dad, Chris, mum, Jacquie, and brother and best mate, Ben. Their endless support is the reason this dream is all possible.

Although my name might be on the front cover of this book, I'm only a small part of the process. Countless hours of labour went into creating something I am truly proud of. Thanks to Jane Wilson, Emily Hart and the Hardie Grant team for creating a book that was home-cook ready while showcasing my chef skills. It was a balancing act that not many could have gotten right, so thank you. Nina Rousseau for the copywriting that blends expert travel dude with cool chef. Deb Kaloper and Bec Hudson for the styling and photography: they are extremely talented and a dream to work with, making the shoot the most enjoyable week of this whole process. Valerie Restarick for all your incredible ceramics that feature in this book and that get used day in and day out at Atlas Dining. Ali Hiew for the editorial skills. And Vincent Casey for working through a few creative challenges and delivering an incredibly original design!

I would also like to acknowledge the staff at Atlas Dining who have helped me with the book and preparation. My team is my backbone, Anna and Victor in particular.

Index

**Published in 2019 by Hardie Grant Books,
an imprint of Hardie Grant Publishing**

Hardie Grant Books (Melbourne)
Building 1, 658 Church Street
Richmond, Victoria 3121

Hardie Grant Books (London)
5th & 6th Floors
52–54 Southwark Street
London SE1 1UN

hardiegrantbooks.com

Photo credits: page 54: Anita Martingano/
Shutterstock.com; page 76: milansys/iStock.com;
page 77: Joel Carillet/iStock.com and nabeel
palliveedu/Shutterstock.com.

This book uses 15 ml (½ fl oz) tablespoons;
cooks with 20 ml (¾ fl oz) tablespoons should
be scant with their tablespoon measurements.

A catalogue record for this
book is available from the
National Library of Australia

The Atlas Cookbook
ISBN 978 1 74379 538 5

10 9 8 7 6 5 4 3 2 1

Publishing Director
Jane Willson

Project Editor
Emily Hart

Editor
Allison Hiew

Design Manager
Jessica Lowe

Designer
Vincent Casey

Writer
Nina Rousseau

Photographer
Bec Hudson

Stylist
Deborah Kaloper

Production Manager
Todd Rechner

Production Coordinator
Mietta Yans

Colour reproduction
by Splitting Image
Colour Studio

Printed in China by
Leo Paper Products LTD.